How Can I Make What I Cannot See?

How Can I Make What I Cannot See?

by **Shiro Fukurai**

Translated by Margaret Haas
and Fusako Kobayashi

Photographs by **Kenji Ishiguro**

Van Nostrand Reinhold Company

New York   Cincinnati   Toronto   London   Melbourne

Jacket and frontispiece:
This brush drawing by a blind girl, entitled
Man Riding a Horse, was warmly received and published in
an article in "Du," a well-known Swiss art magazine.

Van Nostrand Reinhold Company International Offices:
London   Toronto   Melbourne
Van Nostrand Reinhold Company Regional Offices:
New York   Cincinnati   Chicago   Millbrae   Dallas

Copyright © Shiro Fukurai 1969
First published by Kodansha, Tokyo
Translation copyright © 1974 by Litton Educational Publishing, Inc.
Library of Congress Catalog Card Number 73-1623
ISBN 0-442-22490-7

Published in the United States of America in 1974 by
Van Nostrand Reinhold Company
A division of Litton Educational Publishing, Inc.
450 West 33rd Street, New York, N. Y. 10001

1   3   5   7   9   11   13   15   16   14   12   10   8   6   4   2

Library of Congress Cataloging in Publication Data

Fukurai, Shiro, 1920-
How can I make what I cannot see?

Translation of Mitakotonai mon tsukurarehen.
1.   Blind — Education — Art.   I.   Title.
HV1664.A75F913   371.9′11′4   73-1623
ISBN 0-442-22490-7

Contents

For the Reader

"Can the blind really create things?"
"No, it's impossible."
"I've never heard that before."

People who can see find it hard to believe that blind children are also able to create things of artistic merit.

Since 1950, I have been teaching art at Kobe Municipal School for the Blind. My experience there stressing the medium of clay has proven that doubts like those expressed above are wrong. I can now say with certainty that children who are blind also make impressive works, sometimes better than those of children with normal vision.

Such an endeavor is said to be unprecedented in the history of education for the blind. For me, it was the start of a new life adventure.

Part 1 of this book, "The Record of the Soil," is an account of my blind students' progress from their first expressions in clay to their later work in drawing.

Part 2, "Fish that Have Hands," explains and illustrates congenitally blind children's first attempts in clay during my second year of teaching. Encouraging them to do such work was indeed a difficult task. These figures show how hard the children worked to learn clay sculpting. Anything they wished to re-create they had to do with only the knowledge of a part or parts of that object, never comprehending the whole shape of the original. The works also show, however, that these handicapped children have both creativity and normal perceptive powers. I personally am impressed by the strength and faithfulness of their conceptions, not to mention their courage to create.

In addition, I have listened to the children's conversations. Part 3, "A World Without Light," records comments that have impressed me. Their words are light and humorous, and teach us to change our views of the blind. They tell us, for instance, how the blind conceive of space. Please remember that the main characters in most conversations are blind children and that they are usually conversing with weak-sighted children. ("Weak-sighted" refers to those whose eyesight is between 0.04 and 0.3 with glasses and both eyes open. Vision of 0.04 means that one can distinguish the fingers of a hand six feet away.) Because weak-sighted persons can see a little, their way of recognizing things resembles that of a person with normal vision. I feel that the contrasts between these two different worlds will be of special interest.

Recently the number of weak-sighted children in proportion to the number of totally blind children attending schools for the blind is increasing. Therefore, the occasions to hear what the completely blind have to say are decreasing. I fervently hope that this book will be the last one having to record the comments of the blind.

The school in which I work is a small building with Kobe seaport to the south and Mt. Rokko to the north. I teach first- through ninth-graders, two hours a week for each grade. There are forty pupils in the primary school and thirty in the junior-high school.

I would be truly happy if this little book could speak for the blind children in Japan, and I would like to express my thanks to you readers whom I come to know through this book.

I Want Eyes!
by Kiyoshi Mizohata (seventh-grade boy)

After an unsuccessful eye operation, this boy poured his anguish into this sculpture. Although the figure's closed eyes and lax mouth suggest a sense of despair, the outstretched hands reveal that the fervency of his hope remains undiminished.

Children's Work

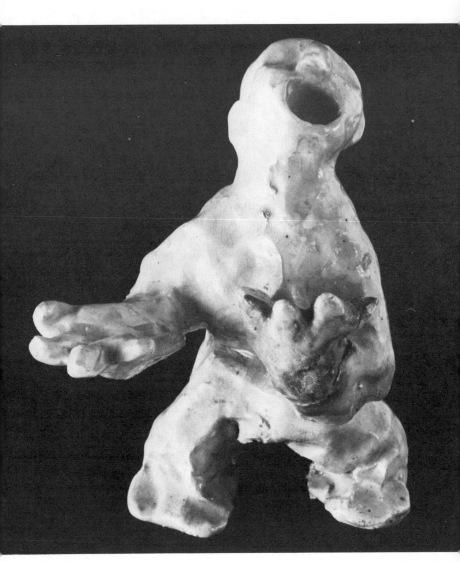

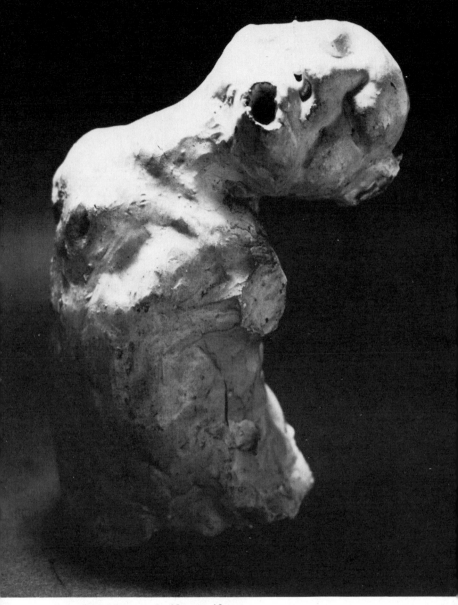

A Blind Person Is Always Alone
by Tsugu Kagimoto (ninth-grade boy)

Hollow eyes and lifeless open mouth. A wandering masseur's expression of loneliness when he stops playing his flute and looks up into the night sky. The face looks like the artist's. This sculpture was returned to Tsugu after being shown in an art exhibit because no one bid for it. The loneliness this work expresses makes me worry deeply about this boy.

O Lord, Please Listen to Me
by Keiko Kawai (eighth-grade girl)

Since this girl had lost the use of the right side of her body, she made this with only her left hand.

The arms of this figure in prayer are proportionately large and the fingers carefully molded one by one. Working the clay with one hand was understandably very difficult, and this work was made after a series of unsuccessful attempts. It took her one hour. This piece was presented to the Pope.

Mother Is Gentle and a Child Sleeps in Her Arms

by Shigenori Matsui (Blind, deaf, and dumb boy, ninth grade)

The mother's hair has a lovely rhythmic quality to it. Her tender look and the child's comfortable sleep are expressed well together. Usually such a complicated combination like this is very difficult for the blind. This is really a masterpiece of the sort that appears only once every ten years or so. Shigenori received the Minister of Welfare Prize.

My Father's Hands Were Big When He Held Me

by Shigeru Kinoshita (eighth-grade boy)

The father's large face and deep eyes express love and strength. The child has no arms or legs but it is somehow a lovely lump. This can be regarded as a work very characteristic of the blind in that it inspires us to handle it in order to appreciate it.

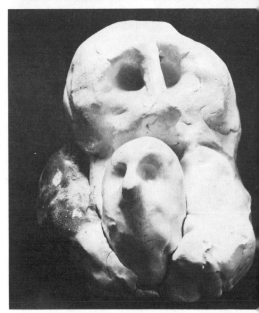

This work is an earlier work by the same artist who did *Mother Is Gentle and a Child Sleeps in Her Arms* (opposite). Both works are detailed designs of a mother and a child, quite different from the abstract art that blind children frequently make.

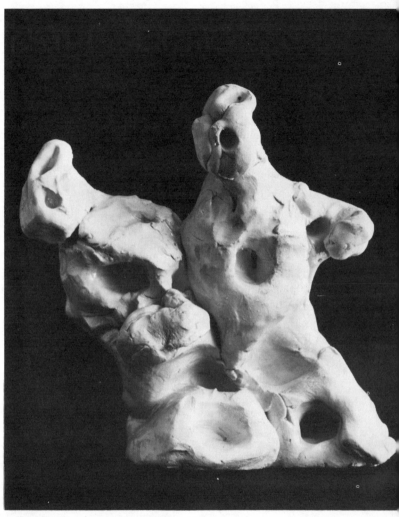

Always a Couple When We Run
by Shojiro Nakamura (sixth-grade boy)

When the children at our school play tag on the playground, a weak-sighted child holds hands with a totally blind child, and they run together. This work shows the inharmonious movement of the two, the leader and the follower. Several deep finger indentations make it a dynamic, unified whole.

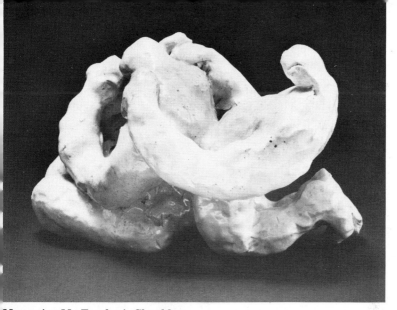

Massaging My Teacher's Shoulders
by Hiroshi Nemoto (ninth-grade boy)

Originally Hiroshi hadn't wanted to become a masseur, but as commencement day approached, he finally must have made up his mind.

"*Sensei* (teacher), I'll give you a massage."

"Oh, thanks, will you?"

"*Sensei,* your shoulders have gotten pretty stiff."

"Oh, really?"

I Will Become a Masseur When I Grow Up
by Kunihiro Momihara (sixth-grade boy)

The long neck of the person being massaged as well as the inclination of the masseur's neck are realistically portrayed. The stick-like construction is technically characteristic of a beginner's work but in this work, it is effective in suggesting the bone structure.

15

A Horseback Rider Raises His Hand
by Hiroyoshi Iida (ninth-grade boy)

The long lump looks more like an abstract animal form than a horse, and it has deep-set eyes and mouth. The sculptor-rider looks happy with his hand up. The strong strokes of the fingers are unexpectedly effective in revealing the inner feelings of the artist. This work was accepted in an art exhibition of the handicapped.

A Winter Night, Mother's Asleep, I Am Awake
by Hiroko Nishi (fourth-grade girl)

Mother has fallen asleep over me; I am awake. Memory of a winter night. The mother also has eyes but they cannot be seen in the photograph. Although simply composed, this work evokes the feeling of warm embrace.

I Want To Be a Mother and Hold a Child
by Toshiko Fukui (fifth-grade girl)

When Toshiko, who has lost her father, is asked what she wants to be when she grows up, always answers "a mother." In general, when two or more human figures are combined in a work, it is very difficult to express the different sizes and forms together. The volume of these artless forms is somehow inspiring.

The Feel of an Insect I Touched Somewhere
by Yukio Hamada (sixth-grade boy)

He has not forgotten the feel of an insect that he timidly touched. The gouge strokes of the fingers of both hands express the movements of the insect. Two holes on the head are the eyes. This is one of the unique themes.

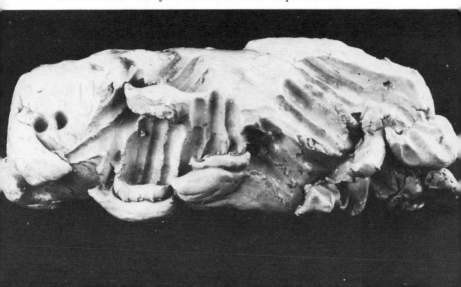

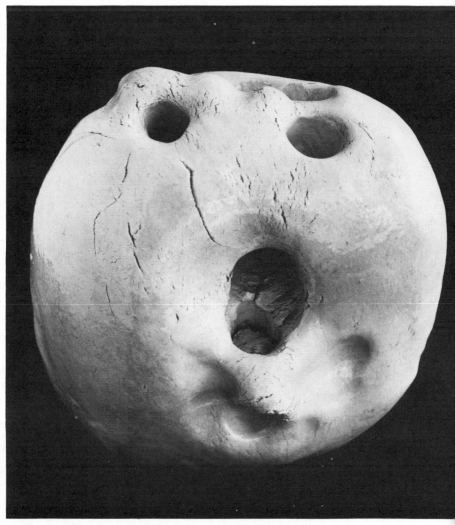

A Face Is Round and There Are Holes in the Eyes and Nose
by Tadao Kumagai (seventh-grade boy)

He described a friend's face that he touched as "round and had holes all over," a very different perception from that of a sighted person. The bridge of the nose is too difficult a construction for him. The skin of this face is smooth and beautiful.

The artist was born without eyeballs.

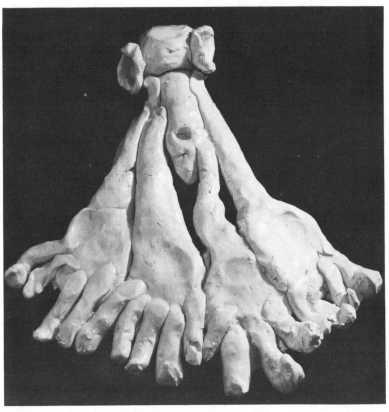

Man's Hands and Feet Are Full of Fingers and Toes
by Hiroko Nishi (fourth-grade girl)

The ears here are especially large in proportion to the other features of the head. The torso in the center of the work is shorter than the length of the arms, and the two legs are together and flanked by the arms. The artist says fingers and toes are "lovely because they are small and move." This work clearly shows the relative degrees of importance with which the artist views the different parts of the body.

Do You See That I Am Furious?
by Shozo Orino (fourth-grade boy)

A weak-sighted child told this artist that if he put his fingers in his mouth and stretched it, he could make a scary face. When he did so on this figure, the face stretched out to the width of the cylinder body. The small projections at the bottom are feet. Thus, subtle movements of the fingers are enough to create very different expressions.

A Child at His Mother's Breasts
by Masamichi Yatsuse (fifth-grade boy)

Just like newborn puppies groping for the mother dog's teats while their eyes are still closed, blind babies rely on their sense of smell and their fingers to find their mother's breasts.

The mother's arms supporting the child here are strong and sturdy. She is like a mother mole with its young.

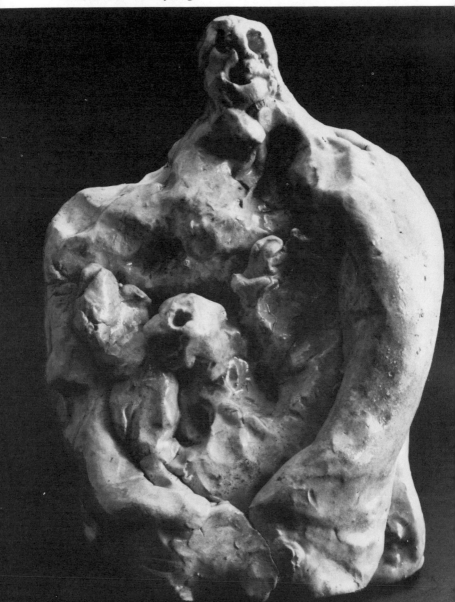

The Warmth of Mother's Baby
by Yoshio Hayakawa (fifth-grade boy)

A baby receives his mother's warmth through her embrace, and within this warmth, the child grows. The mother's quiet happiness appears in her serene smile.

My Father
by Hideyoshi Sayo (sixth-grade boy)

Hideyoshi's father works on the railroad. Hideyoshi still remembers how his father used to carry him to the public bath on his big muscular shoulders. He felt very comfortable there.

This picture shows one portion of a sculpture sixteen inches high.

Run, Pony, Run
by Kiyotoshi Nakao (third-grade boy)

A pony is galloping through the fields with Kiyoshi, the artist. The two holes at the top are the rider's eyes. The horse's four legs are at the bottom, and just beneath the rider's left hand is the pony's small head. The dynamic finger carving shows the fast speed at which they are moving.

Fish
by Etsuko Shirai (fourth-grade girl)

Etsuko molded her fish into a basic stick shape. She added two balls on top of the head as eyes. In the center, she made two flat disk shapes, like human lips, for its mouth. Then she tapered the tail part and added small disks for the scales.

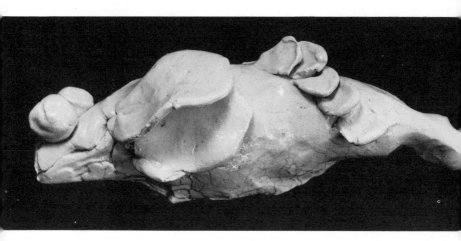

A Dog Walking
by Tsuyoshi Kiso (fourth-grade boy)

When a blind child touches a real dog, this is how he perceives its body. Looking down at his sculpture, the legs are to the left and the right of the dog's back. The hole in the head, the dog's open mouth, is shaped like a man's mouth. The parts difficult to understand are always drawn from human models.

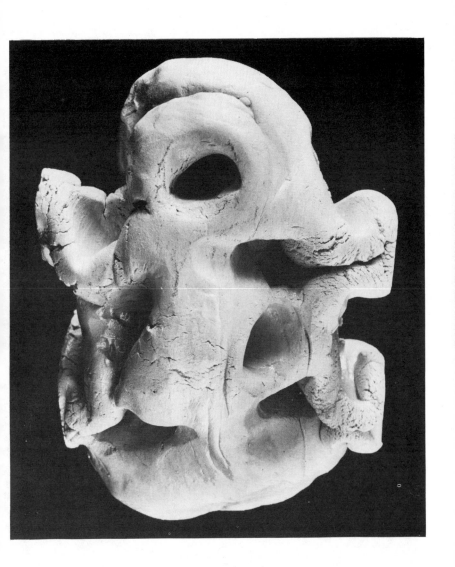

Where Did My Hair Go?
by Yaeko Sumiya (ninth-grade girl)

This girl who touched my head must have thought she would be bald some day. She humorously titled this as "teacher's unexpected surprise." And then giggling, she added, "*Sensei* (teacher), don't be mad!"

Mother's Hands
by Yatsuko Shingawa (first-grade girl)

The sweet smell of mother's breasts, her gentle voice, and her arms compose this figure of mother for a young child. The little girl peeks out from the mother's arms with a lively, funny expression on her face. The two dots at the top are the mother's eyes. As in many works, the faces and the arms are one continuous piece.

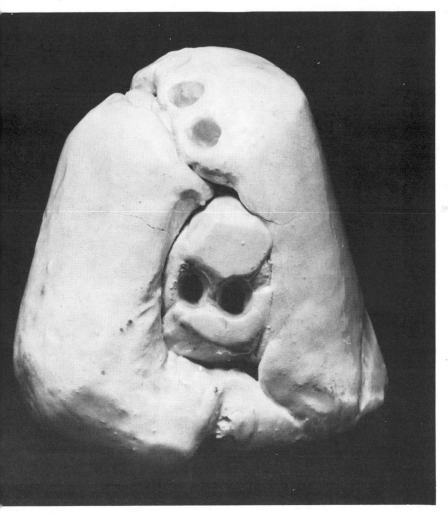

Joy, Happiness

Man Riding A Horse

Mother's Arms

I Want Eyes (written in Japanese characters)

Freeing A Bird

1
The Record of the Soil

The Red Clay 1950

In January of 1950, I lost my job as an art designer. It was five years after the war, and the small newspaper I was working for found it could not make ends meet. I applied to the Kobe City Board of Education for a junior-high-school teaching post. I was then thirty.

I waited impatiently for two long months, and still no answer came. Because the annual official announcement of those selected would soon appear in the newspapers, I decided to go to the City Hall to find out what had happened.

A clerk in charge finally located my application amidst a huge stack of papers.

"You will not be hired," he said.

"Why? Isn't there any school that would take me? Isn't there anything you can do for me?" I suddenly felt dizzy with indignation and frustration.

"It was decided this year that people without the proper educational background would not be accepted. I can't do anything about it."

A change in the educational system after the war meant that my certificate as an art instructor held only half of its former value. Without the required certificate, I could not argue with him.

An opportunity to make my mother happy vanished. When I went home, all I could tell her was that I had not been accepted.

Then I left again to climb the hills behind the house. That day I saw neither the spring sunshine nor the wildflowers by the roadside. I lay down on the bank of the reservoir where I always went when I wanted to be alone. As I thought of my mother's quiet profile, my eyes began to fill with tears. My failure began to seem the natural outcome of not having gone into industry after studying machines at a technical high school. The clear sky above seemed to reflect my despair; the white clouds had dissolved and disappeared just as my wish had.

My desire to be with children was still so strong that I finally sent another application to the City Hall—this time to be a custodian—only to find, however, that I was too late to get a job.

My prewar educational background had brought me to this impasse. Although I kept telling myself I should abandon my desire to work with children, I was finding it very difficult.

I wondered why I liked children so much. Maybe because I was a child myself. Or maybe because I wished to stay one.

More than ten days passed as I tried to give up my wish to be a teacher. Then one evening I received word that the principal of Kobe Municipal School for the Blind had been trying to find me. Wondering what his purpose could possibly be, I went to see him right away. He quietly began to explain.

"Would you consider coming to our school and teaching art?"

"I'm afraid I've had no experience in this sort of work....I don't think I can do it."

The principal was obviously eager to have me join his school. He told me that he had dedicated his life to educating the blind. He explained how important handcrafts were to their education and how urgently he needed an art teacher. His world, however, still seemed completely removed from my own.

"Could I have a night to think about it?" I hardly knew what to think. The offer was so unexpected. No matter how hard I thought about it, it was still impossible to imagine the world of children unable to see.

Finally, after careful consideration, I phoned the principal at noon the next day.

"I have really thought about your offer, but the more deeply I think about it, the less I feel I could teach art to blind children. I'm sorry to disappoint you."

"Mothers become mothers after they give birth to their children," he said gently. "Nobody knows beforehand how to bring them up. Babies teach mothers what they need to know. Won't you try to think about it again?"

Confident that I had made a sincere decision, I was not receptive to his efforts to change my mind. In the following days, however, I started recalling his comments. Over and over they crossed my mind. At last, five days after my phone call to the school, I went to tell him that I had reconsidered after all.

"Could you try to use me?" I inquired in a tense voice.

Thus I was rescued from my crisis. I was to be a teacher after all.

My acquaintance with the principal, Mr. Hideo Imai, started then, and he continued to encourage me until he retired in 1968.

"Tomorrow, be at school at nine o'clock. Please dress suitably for the occasion." This note arrived in the middle of April, rather late for the beginning of a new school term.*

Trembling more with apprehension than excitement, I walked along the narrow path to the school. The main gate of our school was located at the back entrance of an elementary school. I wondered if the original school building had been destroyed in the war, for it was haphazardly located in two old wooden buildings. What impressed me more was the unusual sense of quiet. There was no sign of schoolchildren anywhere.

I was ushered into the principal's room. While waiting there, I had to fight down a strong desire to run away. The principal entered the room, lit a cigarette, and inhaled deeply. "Now that you have come to this school, please avoid the word *blind*." I didn't quite understand what he meant then.

I was expected to formally greet the students, but when the principal led me before everyone lined up by the wisteria tree, I couldn't think of a thing to say. A new teacher lacking self-confidence could hardly hope to make an impressive speech. I could only tell them what I did know to be true.

"Creating things is a thrilling experience. I believe this is the same for everybody. But I don't know anything about you all. Please teach me what your world is like. And in return, I'll try very hard to understand it."

Still groping for the right words, I somehow finished my talk.

*Publisher's note: The Japanese school year begins in early spring.

Their faces showed no response at all. I drew a deep breath and studied my future students more closely. The girl right in front of me looked down at the ground with gray, protruding eyeballs. The one next to her didn't seem to have eyes at all. Even the children with weak eyesight didn't seem to see me. One boy kept moving his head from left to right. What was he thinking? My uneasiness only increased as I looked around at the blank expressions of these unfortunate children of every age and size.

When the bell rang on my first day of school, I nervously gathered up paper and scissors and went off to find my class.

One large classroom had been partitioned into smaller rooms with about six students in each class. When I walked in, they were all seated as though bound to their chairs. The windows were tall and the room gloomy, as though the sunlight was not needed.

"What did you do during the war? What can you make? What do you think you'd like to do?"

I asked every class the same questions. Some children looked at the ground, others touched their desks with their foreheads, but no one answered. In the ninth-grade class, the oldest girl voiced the general opinion.

"We had to evacuate the city so we weren't able to do anything."

For each grade there was only one class, and within each class there were big differences in the ages and levels of the students' intelligence. Most of the children were totally blind, although there were some who were "weak-sighted" or "semi-blind" (eyesight under 0.03).

I started my first class by having the junior-high students fold and cut out pieces of colored paper. The response, however, was discouraging.

"Paste makes my eyes smart."

"I don't know where to make the next fold."

"I can't, it's too difficult."

Even after I simplified the work to kindergarten level, the complaints continued.

The hardest ones to reach were the totally blind children whose expressionless faces never registered what they were thinking. I had no way at all of checking how much they did understand. I also had no idea how developed their sense of touch was or how to improve my own. There were other bewildering aspects too. One boy who put his fingers in his eyes, and rocked back and forth especially troubled me. To whatever I asked him, he could only stammer "haa, haa" in reply.

Why was it that these children who played and laughed so merrily during recess turned silent and unresponsive in the classroom?

The children's sense of touch was highly developed but they had never been taught how to make things with their hands. Although special education for the blind began in Kyoto in 1878, art instruction was rarely offered in schools for the blind. In fact, late one night the principal told me that the institutions for helping the blind had only really become schools after the war. Until then some children had even had to beg at stations with signs around their necks.

I desperately wanted to teach these children how to create art with their hands but I had no idea where to begin. With no example to follow, I went about my teaching feeling bewildered and directionless.

A month passed. One day I stood by a classroom window pondering the problem. As I looked out toward the north, I could dimly see the mountains over the rubber factory. They fascinated me as they changed color according to the time of day, sometimes seeming far away, sometimes right nearby. Perhaps if I went to the top of one of those mountains, I would feel inspired.

The sky was blue and a soft summer breeze was blowing as I made my way up the narrow path, pushing aside the overgrowth as I went. When I reached the mountain top and looked down into the valley, my eyes caught a sharp glint of light. It was sunlight reflecting off the surface of a small pond. I hurried down the steep incline to explore it. Not a ripple disturbed the calm, deep green surface of the water that mirrored the majestic beauty of the surrounding pines.

As I walked along the edge, I noticed that my feet, sinking into wet ground, had uncovered a red layer hidden under the gray topsoil. I scooped up a handful and rolled it in my hands. It was soft yet resilient and easily turned into a smooth round ball. "It is clay! Pure clay!" I told myself as a new idea flashed through my mind. Why hadn't I realized that paper was an inanimate medium for my children. I should use a lively substance like clay!

I found an old desk in the school backyard that could be used as a work table. As I repaired it, I felt hopeful for the first time since I started to teach. "Those hands will create something, something wonderful! Just as people say, they must have a keenly developed sense of touch."

The first class to try using the clay was thirteen-year-old junior-high boys and girls. With a heap of red clay in front of me, I gathered the six students around the work table.

"I have something new for you today and I hope you will like it," I said. "It is clay, and it can be molded into all sorts of forms. Use your imagination. Express your feelings in shapes. Feel it and try to make something with it."

As though there were a secret agreement among them, nobody reached out for the clay.

"I have never done it before!"

"It's impossible. How can I make what I cannot see?"

"What's the use of doing it? The blind don't need to do things like that."

"In the end we'll only be blind masseurs."*

To my surprise, one after another, they spit bitter words at me. And to these words, I had no answer. "How can I make what I cannot see?" As this phrase went round and round in my mind, the children left one by one. The last girl to leave turned around and shouted, "Be blind, then you'd know."

After this, the attitude of the older students hardened toward me. They started to mock my efforts to convince them to work with the clay.

"I know you're blind but you can talk, you can imagine things you can't see. You have two good hands. Do something with them."

"But, do you really know what it's like to be blind?"

"Why did he come to our school?"

"He probably had no other place to go."

They made fun of me, and it was getting steadily worse. The other teachers were all old men who didn't seem to care how classes were taught. Because I was desperate, I asked them for

*Publisher's note: In Japan, blind people are frequently employed as masseurs.

advice. One told me to take my time. Another teacher, a sixty-year-old blind man, simply said, "Wait until you hit the bottom, become pessimistic, and learn to accept the blind as blind. Then you may know how to really try and help them. Or it may be that you only become resentful of them. But you do know, don't you, that no one has ever done what you are doing now?"

A Quiet Confrontation 1951-54

The gloomy year finally passed, and the strong summer sunlight reached the dark corners of the school corridor again.

I was certain after all that clay was the only medium through which the children could freely express themselves. I knew they had to construct their own sense of reality as they perceived it. I was sure now that I was taking the right road.

Once again, I placed the clay on the work table in the end of the corridor.

It was time for the third-graders' class. I took a small piece of clay and put it in one child's hands. Then I guided his hands to show him how to knead it.

"Now, this is the clay. Here, try and feel it."

"Ugh, it feels really cold and strange."

"It is clammy and feels awful."

"Is it all right to hold it? Won't it move?"

"It smells like a snail."

One child touched it gently with his fingertips, and a smile appeared on his face. Another brought his nose to the clay. Another stuck a finger into her piece of clay and kept it there. Another pinched off bit after bit and dropped them on the floor.

One healthy-looking boy was already energetically molding the clay. When I asked him what he was making, he said, "You shouldn't look at what I'm doing. Please go away." He turned his back to hide his work from me.

To my relief, they were touching the clay after all.

In the second-grade class, I carefully watched a boy who lacked eyeballs from birth. For a while he timidly patted the surface, and leaned over to sniff it, but barely touched it. All of a sudden, he slapped it twice with the palm of his hand. Then, he sighed with relief, "Ah, now, it's dead."

He began to laugh happily. Had he been scared of the clay?

In the third-grader's class, one child made two finger-size sticks, one long, one short, and placed them side by side.

"What are they?"

"A mother snake and a baby snake."

How could she know how a snake was shaped? How could she imagine what she couldn't touch? I could only guess that she had figured this out after hearing snakes described as "long and narrow."

In the fourth-grade class, one blind child showed me a lump of clay with a flat, lid-shaped piece of clay on top of it.

"Guess what this is?" He grinned.

"It's a box, isn't it?"

"No, it's a pit for you to fall into."

With a secret smile, he lifted the lid to reveal a deep yawning hole.

I went to another child and asked, "Is this a person?"

"No, it isn't."

"Then what would it be?"

"*Sensei* (teacher), don't you know what this is? It's a scary monster!"

He showed me a large lump of clay with long scratch marks and holes, and dropped it on the floor with a thud.

"Say you're scared," he said.

A girl with gray eyeballs placed two flat discs of clay on my open palm.

"What is this?" I asked.

"A face."

I had no idea how to interpret these two discs as a face.

Later I found out they represented cheeks.

"*Sensei*, take a look at this." One boy who could see with one of his eyes held a slab of clay against his face and said "boo!"

I could see one of his eyes through a hole in the clay.

Stars, mountains, rivers, gods took forms incomprehensible to me.

"I finished!" one child shouted.

"What have you made?"

"Well . . . ."

"You don't know?"

"I forget."

Some children couldn't even tell me what they had made.

Both elementary and junior-high-school students made the same sort of things. Many of them were things to eat, potatoes, candy, cakes, or things they had touched, cups and bowls, or things they had listened to, such as radios and flutes.

I began to save some of their works, storing them away on shelves in the hall. As I studied them over and over again, I began to notice the following things. (1) The parts of an object that they know and put together are very different from the actual objects themselves. Probably it is very hard for them to envision an entire outline of the objects they wish to represent. (2) Many of the children's versions of actual objects are composed of balls, flat surfaces, and stick shapes. (3) The parts the children know well or are interested in are exaggerated in their proportions. (4) They are very good at expressing the indentations and projections of the real objects. (5) They can easily re-create the rough and smooth textures of surfaces. (6) They can make imaginary things, but these are always based on forms they have touched and felt, especially those of the human body.

Realizing these truths, I came to really understand the parable of the three blind men and the elephant. Works with parts that were lacking or miscombined seemed to have the same feeling as walking in an odd pair of shoes.

I wondered if not being able to see an object always meant that one could not re-create its form exactly. I wondered who had ever said that the blind have keener senses. These works seemed to reveal just the opposite. The so-called extra sensitivity of the blind apparently only meant that they could read braille and walk with canes. On the whole, weren't the creative powers of a blind person inferior? I was finding, after all, that handcrafts were very difficult to do without eyesight.

Were these two long and heavy years only to teach me the limitations of the world of the blind?

With the exception of a few of their efforts in clay which I kept for reference, I decided to destroy all the rest. As I dropped them one by one into a large basin of water, I had to fight down a growing sense of irritation.

Then suddenly one particular clay figure caught my attention. It was made differently from the others. I didn't know what it was supposed to be but I was impressed by the sharp, sensitive modeling technique. Unfortunately, by the time I had discovered it I had sunk almost all of them.

What attracted me to this figure? It struck me as a positive sign, a glimmer of light suddenly coming through a closed door. But I had no idea who had made it.

"Sensei, could you come here a minute?" called a ninth-grade boy who always nodded his head and showed the whites of his eyes as he spoke. His blindness was congenital. I was surprised that he had called me because he usually gave me excuses for not working. The clay figure on his desk was shaped like an airplane, two by three inches.

"What is this?"

"Sensei, you should understand it."

"I wonder what it could be."

"You don't know?"

Silence.

"It's a dog."

"Do you have a dog?"

"Yes, that's why I know what he's like."

"Tell me which part is which?"

"These are his arms and these are his legs. This is the tail."

What he meant by "arms" and "legs" were the front and hind legs of the figure which were attached to the torso as though his

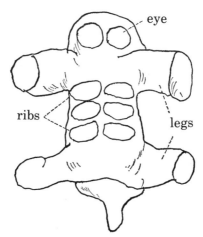

work represented a stretched animal skin.

But what I couldn't understand were six small pieces of clay in two rows along the torso.

"What are these button-like things?"

"Oh, you know, when you pat a dog, you feel them."

"What part of the dog do you mean?"

"Oh, these bumpy places," he said, taking my hand and moving it down one side of his skinny chest. I could feel his ribs.

Those small pieces of clay represented the dog's ribs!

Of course anyone who holds a dog can feel his ribs, although a child with normal vision never tries to express what is beneath the fur. This was the unique understanding, this was the special domain of the blind. I could now see their sightless world. This is what I had been looking for.

I was overjoyed. At the same time, I quietly knew which way I should go.

The little boy remained intrigued with the idea of representing his dog in clay. Several weeks later he brought me another figure. This time it was three-dimensional but its torso made it look like a desk with crooked legs.

"Because he gallops as he runs, his hind legs must be longer than his front legs . . . ."

Once again before he graduated, he brought me a clay dog, again one with long hind legs. Soon after he left the school, he died. But the first work he had left me was what inspired me to go on teaching the blind. I still have that work. And because of it, I started once again to collect my children's works, this time with clear vision and purpose.

One day in May, as I considered the children's progress with small clay objects over a half-year, I began to wonder how well they could perceive objects much larger than themselves.

"Do you know what a horse is like?" I asked the seventh-graders' class.

"I touched one in the countryside. He was like short, withered grass in the fields."

"One day walking along a street, I bumped into a very big person. I apologized, and people started to laugh at me. I asked them why. No wonder it was so funny. I had walked into a horse. I was surprised at how enormous he was." He giggled.

Their experiences with horses were after all much like those of the blind men and the elephant.

There was a pause in the conversation. Then Tadashige Uchikawa, a totally blind boy, began to talk.

"*Sensei*, I know how a horse is shaped."

"How do you know?"

"When I was small, I touched a toy horse with a warrior doll on top of it. It was a decoration for Boy's Festival.*"

"Do you still remember its shape?"

"Yes, I do."

"Tadashige, I'd like to see the horse that you know. Will you try to make it? How about it?"

"Yes, I will try to do it."

He began to work on his horse.

"Tadashige, make it as you recollect it. Rely only on yourself and your ideas. Feel confident to make your own horse," I told him, and then carefully watched the movement of his fingers at work. I was hoping to discover some hints on how to teach my students better.

He didn't hesitate as he shaped and molded one part of the horse from a big lump of clay. I was deeply impressed by his hands, which he moved as though he were using his eyes.

"*Sensei*, let me work on this project until I'm satisfied with it," he said and continued to work on the horse day after day.

At first he seemed to have trouble relating his mental concepts of what he wanted to express to his hand movements. Gradually, he transferred his focus from working on only part of the horse to working on the horse as a whole figure. As his understanding deepened, his hands began to move faster and faster.

"*Sensei*, look! I did it!" It was the end of September. The finished horse had a mane like a girl's long hair and an indescribable, enchanting air. He never tried to make a horse again, as though he were afraid he could not make another like it.

The horse was so unique that I decided to present it to the Japanese branch of UNESCO. A short while later, we were informed that Tadashige's horse would receive the UNESCO Art Prize. I could hardly believe it. One mild day in October of the same year, Tadashige and I went to receive the prize in a happy daze.

*Publisher's note: Japanese families with sons celebrate Boys' Festival Day by decorating a room with warrior dolls and toy armour, hoping their sons will grow up into sturdy, brave men.

The story appeared in big articles in the newspapers. It was unprecedented for a blind child to receive an art prize. Suddenly the atmosphere at the school became vivacious. "I, too, want to be like Tadashige!" the children responded, as each touched and felt the trophy and handed it to the next child. It became a source of hope for everyone.

"Tadashige, you did very well. I didn't help you at all."

"*Sensei*, what on earth are you saying. I could make it because you encouraged me."

I could only squeeze his hand very tightly.

Shortly afterward, he was killed in an accident. For me, however, his spirit still lives on in the clay, a source of encouragement when I get discouraged.

The deep impression Tadashige's success made upon the children lasted quite a while. With this success too, I was finally accepted as a teacher. As a result, however, I felt more bewildered than before because I still did not know how to guide my students.

Then in the seventh-graders' class, I first noticed that their enthusiasm had faded. Something was disturbing them.

"*Sensei*, was Tadashige really good or . . . ?"

"Didn't they give him the prize out of sympathy?"

"It's obvious children who can see are better in art than we are, isn't it?"

Even though I emphatically denied it, the children all began striking their desk tops and expressing their doubts in louder and louder voices.

"*Sensei*, how do you know for sure?"

"There is no proof for what you say, no proof. . . ."

"That's right. There isn't, *Sensei*."

I had no sure way of proving to them that what they said was wrong. The seeds of doubt grew and spread throughout the school and began to affect the whole student body.

It had never occurred to me that deep in their hearts blind children were very conscious of sighted children. They could not forget that they were sometimes referred to derisively as "blind." By degrees I began to understand that their inferiority complex with respect to the majority of normal-sighted children made them view this prize as given in bad faith.

The history of education for the blind has no record of blind children competing with sighted children in art work. When I realized that my students and I would have to set the precedent, pride and happiness in winning the prize began to fade. Now I would have to find some important, clear evidence that would negate their inferiority complex.

My collection of the children's works already numbered several hundred pieces. Through studying them, I thought I had formulated some sort of fundamental basis for instruction. I decided to teach clay from June to September, and commence with the following exercises.

1) Through singing and dancing, help them acquire a sense of rhythm so that they could move their fingers more dynamically.

2) Expose them to a variety of objects so that they would be able to grasp the entire shape of these real objects and express them.

3) Find themes in blind children's lives and hopes to help them set more specific aims in their work.

Thus wishing to help them make their finger motions dynamic, their posture relaxed and easy, and to instill musical rhythm in their minds, I added a period for song and dance before or after the clay class as well as making simplified animal and human figures to heighten their curiosity and joy in touching things. To teach them to give expression to their daily lives, it was necessary to talk with each of them and to encourage them to develop their imaginations. They had to become good actors, capable of generating inspiration and purpose for their artistic work.

Because they had not been trained this way from their early childhood, these efforts were like building a sand castle at the shore.

Giving Form to Feelings 1956-57

After seven years, the students were finally able to represent things in clay but they were still far from producing lively works of art.

I wondered why. Were they dull and insensitive after all? Hadn't the singing and dancing helped in any way? Does a lack of visual stimulation really make man such an inhibited being? Was it impossible to expect that someday my students would embody their work with lively young feelings? I wasn't looking for special designs or compositions. I was searching for their essence. Once again I thought I had come up against a solid wall.

I recalled how I felt in 1951 when I was dissolving the students' inadequate results and how the forceful cast of that one clay piece had abruptly changed my gloomy outlook. Yet I still wondered how that blind child could have made such a work. His advantage must have been the very strength of not being limited by the sense of vision, something unique of course to the blind. Of course, that is it! I suddenly realized.

Blind people are often regarded as passive. Perhaps it is natural to think that quiet people produce quiet works of art. But let's look at it the other way around. Assume vital works of art are born from quiet people. This is the sort of art I wanted them to bring forth with their hands. This change from stillness to movement would probably turn out to be an internal revolution for these children, and I would have to do it.

Although I was taken with my new idea, when I stood in front of the students, my resolution weakened. I didn't know where to start, and there was no clear guideline at all.

"What's bothering you, *Sensei?*"

"I have something I'd like to ask you all."

"What sort of thing?"

"When you work with clay, why don't you do it with spirit? Are you always like this?"

"We are like wet firewood."

"What does that mean?"

"It means we don't catch fire quickly."

"Then shall I douse you in gasoline?"

"Unfortunately, even if you do so, we won't catch fire easily. We can't help the way we are."

"Yes, that's right," the other students joined in chorus.

When I heard these words, I clapped my hands. That was it. I would be a source of power for them. I would move them, and then the same power would move their hands. Their true selves would appear when they were awakened to a courageous creative attitude which they would receive through my breath, my voice, and my spirit. I was sure their inner selves were not so quiet. Although they tried to be animated, it was hard for them to be that way. Since inspiring works came from a vivacious spirit and body, I decided I would stimulate the children as much as possible. I would become one with the children.

When I realized that sculpture is expressing feelings in concrete form, I finally had the guiding principle I needed. I had studied the blind person's handicaps and felt I had figured out how they could use them in a positive light. Next I had to make sure that the children really understood my idea.

"Up to now, I have learned a great deal from you. From now on, I'd like you to listen to me," I told my students.

"Okay, sure!" they answered cheerfully.

Carefully pronouncing my words, I went on to tell them, "When you work with clay, don't sit down. Work standing up. When you sit down, your spirit does also, and you end up only fooling around with the clay. Don't let your spirit or your body get lazy. Focus your whole body in your fingers and mold it.

"Work with the largest amount of clay possible. Don't lose the fight between it and you. Don't let yourself be defeated.

"Once you start working, don't think you can start all over again. Tell yourself you have one chance to succeed or fail. You can't stop in the middle. Don't waste time in the process.

"Ready, set, charge," I repeated over and over.

I also felt it was important for them to regulate their breathing in order to concentrate steadily on their work.

While they worked and I watched, I ended up taking the same breathing pace that they had. When the children were putting strength into their work, they naturally voiced sounds, "Yah, yo, yo-ho," to increase their concentration and encourage each other.

In my concern, I responded with the children as they pulled and stretched the clay. I think mothers who are toilet-training their children follow them in exactly the same way.

In June, I narrowed the students' subject matter to focus only on the human body. First, they were to get to know the different parts of body and emphasize the bone and muscle structure in their work. Then they were to continue their practice by making figures expressing the human body in various postures. The children became very interested and learned the names of bones and muscles. However, it wasn't at all easy for them to show their emotions and their intentions through the gestures of their clay figures.

The children used me as a model, and in this way, we got to

know much more about each other.

"*Sensei*, you're tall, aren't you?"

"You're bald. I didn't know that."

Later they moved on from copying models to themes that I gave them. This new direction widened their range of ideas, and as time passed, they made rapid improvement. Their fortes were themes such as mother and child, brothers, masseurs, and figures reading braille.

In the quiet classroom, after school, whenever I carefully examined these simple yet daring works, I felt as though I were opening thrilling mystery boxes.

One day in October of 1956, I noticed a big poster in a shop window on my way home. It was about an art contest for children, held under the auspices of the junior division of the Nikaten Art Exhibition. In western Japan, every art-inclined elementary and junior-high student aspires to enter this most authoritative children's exhibition.

As I read on, my eyes caught sight of a sculpture section, and all of a sudden my heart began to beat faster. In the previous years, they had only had a division for painting. "This is it! Children, this is the chance you've been waiting for!" I murmured to myself.

Carefully I started considering this event.

I had not ever taught my students how to make sculpture especially for exhibition. Although I was a designer, I was only an amateur, neither a sculptor nor a painter. In fact, the entries submitted would probably give me my first opportunity to check and correct my own teaching methods. Apart from that, perhaps all I could do was encourage my students.

At that point, I asked myself how, in fact, the blind children's work compared with the work of sighted children.

1) The blind children's work is without pretensions. It has a fresh sense of forcefulness, perhaps because the students must transfer their feelings directly from their hands to the clay.

2) Even though their work is inevitably simple and naive, these qualities do not reduce its value. Rather, their art can be interpreted as life in its concentrated essence.

3) Since the children cannot imitate someone else's style, each one reveals his own individuality. The expressive surfaces of their sculpture, which strongly appeal to the sense of touch, are

very different from the smooth, lifeless surfaces of the graveside *haniwa* statues.* I wonder if it isn't possible to say that their work emphasizes a new tactile dimension in artistic beauty which includes a sense of power and movement in its simplicity. I am sure it is also an art form that touches the hearts of many people through the channel of sight.

This is what I believed, and I wanted to find out if it was true.

By October 10, 1956, the entries had to be finished. Therefore, I told my eighth-grade class, "Now, could I have everybody's attention? Please, don't be surprised, but let's try to send the work you do in today's class to an art museum in Osaka. This exhibition is for the children of western Japan. If your art is accepted, then your doubts and feelings of inferiority will melt away, you will gain confidence, and the younger students who follow you will have hope. But I will send only three pieces, not everyone's. Now, start working, and do your best."

"Oh, yes. I was waiting for this," said one boy.

Six of the students were smiling. Nobody seemed confused by my idea. Each student began vigorously kneading his clay. Gradually a sense of tension filled the classroom.

"Well, are you ready? These past seven years of effort were all for today. I have nothing more to tell you. Take your time to decide what you're going to make. Use my body or a friend's for help in what you are trying to make. What's important is to follow your emotions as they lead you through the clay. How you indent is important, but don't make meaningless strokes. Absorb yourself in the clay. Now, are you ready?"

"Let's go, I'm gonna do it."

"Just watch me, I'll do it."

"Here I go! Yeah!"

Using the sort of shouts and cries normally used only in sports, each projected his spirit into his work. I carefully watched each one of them.

One child started working from the top part of a tall lump of clay on the work table. It was a human body. He made the neck distinct from the head by pinching the clay between his thumb and forefinger. With his finger tips, he made the face and the delicate details of the hair. Then, below the neck, he hollowed out a place to add a long roll of clay to fit in the shoulders and form

*Publisher's note: Clay funerary statues placed in prehistoric tombs as dedicatory objects.

the arms. Molding with the palm of his hand and pressing with his thumbs, he worked on the bulges and hollows of the arm muscles. The chest, the back, and the stomach were conceived as one piece. Each move was final and decisive, and he never went back to work over any part. His fingers gripped, stretched, pushed, hollowed, strongly, lightly, quickly, slowly. Then he divided the bottom part of the clay into two portions and attached two rolls of clay to start the legs.

The subtle motions of his hands carved waves in the clay. The figure was given an active posture. His own creation, his unique interpretation, had to come from how he himself responded to the actual object he had touched.

Tense breathing and the whoosh of clay being kneaded were the only sounds in the room. The students' hands moved as though they were filled with separate life. Molding the clay with all their strength, it only took each of them thirty minutes to complete their sculptures.

"I've done it!" they were cheerfully shouting, one after another. I walked around the room and paused in front of each creation. The feelings of each individual artist were clearly expressed on the surface of that person's particular sculpture. Then how about the themes? The total shape? The expression? Were there any unnecessary places? Any messy finger traces? I evaluated each piece as though it were reflected on the mirror of my own spirit. I faced them as though they were Buddhist statues, and I were drawing life from them. I viewed the whole to its parts, the parts to the whole, and in so doing the shape of each work gave way to its essence.

"The shapes are good. The finger traces are effective and the expressions are good. They are impressive! Yes, they are touching! You all did a very fine job. Masterpieces!" I told them in a loud voice and patted them on the shoulders.

Each work of art was so powerful that it was almost impossible for me to select the best three.

Long afterwards, the classroom's tense atmosphere filled with students' enthusiastic shouting and energetic hand movements seemed to linger on.

Several days had passed, and still the clay pieces were not dry, so I was finding it hard to stay calm. Before I sent them to the exhibition, I still had to fire them twice, first unglazed and then with glaze. At last, the day for glazing came and I put them in the firing oven. After nine long hours, I looked at the color of the fire through the peep hole, and it seemed just the right time to take out the clay.

As I opened the lid of the furnace, heat flooded my face and at first I could not insert the tongs. I held my breath and drew out the finished pieces. They changed from yellow to red, to dark red, and then were swallowed up in the darkness. I suddenly felt chilly alone in the October night.

It was already dawn when I took a taxi home, carefully holding the sculpture on my lap. "Are my own eyes really unerring in their judgment? I wonder if it isn't contradictory to visually evaluate what has been created by those who can only see with their hands."

As they had for many months before, these questions continued to spin through my mind.

After the entries had been sent to the museum, I remember that my resolution began to waver.

Several days later around noon time the phone rang.

"Is it your school? The one which sent us those clay sculptures?"

"Yes, that's right," I answered.

"Well, they're all accepted for the exhibition."

"What? Oh, really? Are you really sure?"

The judges had been speechless when they first saw the children's unusual work. The students had succeeded in very keen competition. Only one out of every thirty was accepted. Thus they were proudly selected and ranked with children who could see.

"Thank you, thank you very much," I said, pressing my hands together in gratitude.

I gathered my students. "You've all been accepted! Congratulations! You have all worked really hard and you deserve this. Probably no one in the world has done anything like this. Congratulations! My hearty congratulations to you!"

The students broke into applause and loud shouts of joy.

"Wow, I'm happy! I won't complain anymore."

"We're better than children who can see, aren't we?"

"If we try, we too can do things."

"Because our *Sensei* is a good teacher."

"*Sensei*, shake hands with me."

As the children held my hands, I looked up at dark blue Mt. Takatori, remembering seven years ago, with renewed spirit.

The art critic's evaluation in the newspaper gave one sure clue as to my teaching method: "The ability to exactly re-create shapes in clay and the imposing power expressed in the blind children's art opens a new frontier in the world of art."

I Have Touched a Cow, Meditating, Walking in the Wind—these three particularly substantial and expressive pieces of sculpture became sources of hope for all the children at our school as pioneering examples of art created by the blind.

November 4, 1956, is one glorious day in our long and difficult struggle, even though it is probably a day of celebration only for us.

Our first successful art competition not only impressed the students but also gave them self-confidence. Afterwards, no one talked about sighted children anymore, and every fall they competed to see whose work would be accepted.

"It's my turn to get it."

"No, it's my turn. Just be quiet."

"We'll see who's accepted."

"*Sensei*, please teach me how to do it."

I was now able to say that I had fulfilled my promise to the children. I had proved to them that their ability was equal to that of children who could see. I wanted more, however. I wanted each of them to make their own individual demonstration of proof and establish their own sense of confidence. I wanted each child to experience the joy of striving and creating. Thus, we continued to send entries to exhibitions every year. One student's sculptures were accepted four years in a row. A few double-handicapped students also had their work accepted. I have to emphasize that these children were totally blind, completely deprived of sight.

"When we try, we too can make things." It is my hope that their realization of this truth, that blind children stand on an equal basis with sighted children, will remain an encouraging force throughout their lives.

Our record of success is as follows:

1953   Art Prize from Japan UNESCO

1954   The Minister of Welfare Prize in the Japan National Exhibition of the Handicapped

1956   Accepted in the Nikaten Children's Exhibition

1957 The Mayor of Osaka Prize in the Nikaten Children's Exhibition

1958 Accepted in the Nikaten Children's Exhibition.
Accepted in the Dobiten Exhibition of the city of Ashiya

1959 Accepted in the Nikaten Children's Exhibition

1960 Accepted in the Nikaten Children's Exhibition.
Accepted in the Dobiten Exhibition of the city of Ashiya

1961 Accepted in Hyogo Prefecture Exhibition of the Handicapped.
Accepted in the Dobiten Exhibition of the city of Ashiya

With a general understanding of art education in Japanese schools for the blind, I began to wonder about those of foreign countries. Accordingly, I sent inquiries out to over ten countries.

In my questionnaire, I asked how blind children abroad were taught clay modeling and what books they had available on such research.

Almost all the replies I received in the following half year revealed that they had no such special programs or research. Rather they would be interested in my work here.

The only pamphlet I received was from the United States but the artwork pictured was powerless and poorly shaped. Thus, the reports from abroad ended up providing unexpectedly meager results.

I turned to my students.

"Even though you knew you could do it, why didn't you ever try to make things before?"

"Because we thought if people saw them, they would decide as a matter of course that what we made was poorly done. At first, we also thought you were one of those people."

"Oh, so that's why. Do you still feel that way?"

"No, now it's different, but only with *Sensei*."

The more I talked together with the children and understood their individual feelings, the more I understood one particular problem. They were suffering from the scorn with which sighted people treated them. "I can put up with losing my sight but, when I am viewed with contempt, my fervent hopes disappear. Why can't the others understand the feelings of the blind?" they would say.

Whenever I heard this, I became very indignant that there could be such insensitive people.

What kind of Providence determines that I can see and that these children cannot see? What next should I have them do with the clay? Pondering these questions, once again an answer came to me.

What would be the worldly significance, if any, of the fact that some blind children created a few fine works of art? Unless they had the love and understanding of the society around them, they would never be truly happy. We would have our own exhibition and appeal to the public by showing them the creativity of blind children. I could do at least this to answer the children's hopes. Yes, let's have our own exhibit!

Again God had given me a task to do. As my plan to have an exhibition developed, my determination increased.

Renting space somewhere was the next problem. Considering their interest in doing business, I hesitated to ask a department store. But when I gathered my courage and inquired about the possibility, I found a merchant willing to give us display room in one store.

The place was the basement floor of the Daimaru Department Store in Kobe. I displayed a hundred pieces of sculpture and photographs I had taken of the daily life of the children and called it "The Exhibition of Lightless Sculptors."

February 5, 1957, was a dark, cloudy day with occasional rain showers. Even the weather seemed to match the unusual name of the exhibit.

I stood by the entrance and wondered how many people would be interested enough to enter, and if they did so, whether or not they would understand the children's art. But as I started to lose heart, I felt as though I could hear the children's encouraging voices coming to me.

"The Exhibition of Lightless Sculptors" — what is it?"

"Some children who can't see have made dolls. Go and look at them. They're touching. Almost made me cry."

Conversations like this could be heard here and there, and each day the exhibition grew more crowded.

Some people just stood there with tears in their eyes; some, greatly moved, could not leave the place right away.

"I've never heard of children like this before. It's amazing that they can make these works of art. Even people who can see can't make such fine things."

It is impossible to describe just how encouraging these words of love and understanding were.

"Mommy, did you see the one I made?"

"Yes, it was very well done."

The mother's eyes were moist with tears; the child beamed.

"Simple forms with very powerful appeal."

"They have force so near to reality that they can hardly be understood visually."

The comments of art critics began to reveal the true value of this art to the general public. Articles on the exhibition spread widely. They even began to appear abroad, and as a result, the exhibition became known throughout the world.

The exhibition was also held in Kyoto, Tokyo, Nagoya, Hakata, Sasebo, Nagasaki, Oita, Miyazaki, and other places, and finally ended in July of that year after greatly increasing many people's awareness of the blind children's world.

"Up until now I was ashamed that I had a blind child and would always look down at the ground. But when I realized that my child could also do this kind of skilled work, I became hopeful for her future."

When I heard about this mother's reaction to her child's sculpture in the display, I realized that I had been able to render some assistance to the blind, even if only a little, through the exhibition.

Let me quote some more of the comments the viewers made at the exhibit.

"I have seen quite a few exhibitions in the past, but I have never been quite so impressed as I was with this one. I might say that here my eyes finally really began to see. I can't help thinking that for many people, the eyes are only an obstacle to really seeing things."

"I can never forget the joy of looking at such a wonderful art exhibit. 'Wonderful' is the only word to describe it. I was amazed and wondered what we have been seeing up to now with our eyes."

"Although I'm well over fifty years old, I was so impressed I couldn't stop crying for a while. You may wonder why I shed tears. The feelings which pour forth from your work are purifying to my soul."

"I had failed in my business and everything seemed so helpless, I was thinking of dying. But when I saw the things you had expressed so sincerely from the depths of your souls, I began to feel stronger and wanted to try again."

"It is really my first time to see art so beautiful that it reaches the soul. When these figures, so innocently and artlessly created, appeared before me, tears came to my eyes. Each work gives forth the spirit of its maker. I am also struck by the sculptors' abundantly confident attitudes and by their sure expression of emotions. Those who can see tend to be so conscious of other people's eyes that they cannot be really straightforward and open. I believe these are indeed true works of art."

"These figures are not superficially beautiful outlines but are what the children sought for and saw in the eyes of their souls. They are imbued with the deep spirits of their creators. I just can't describe them in words. Dear children, please always continue to do your best to seek beauty, for the world of art is a world without boundaries."

I Want Eyes 1959

In 1959, the second semester had started and art class had begun when I realized that Kiyoshi Mizohata, one of the seventh-graders, was absent. According to one of his friends, he had entered the hospital for an eye operation, but it was hard to imagine that he would regain his eyesight.

Before long, in early October, I came across him in the hall.

"How was it?"

He didn't try to answer. His expression was hard and his way of walking hadn't changed. As I had suspected, the operation had been a failure. Although I knew, I didn't know what to say to comfort him. Later he recorded his feelings of that time as follows.

"The day that I was to leave the hospital arrived. My father consulted the doctor. He replied uneasily, 'I regret to say that he will not be able to see. Please don't be discouraged.'

"I wept in my heart because if I showed it on my face, I would only add to my father's sorrow. The tears continued to fall without end.

" 'Kiyoshi, even though you cannot see you must continue to study hard, okay?' Father said.

"When I get angry with someone, I am scolded. Small kids scorn me as a 'blind.' I wouldn't have to suffer if only I could see. I hate the word 'blind' with all my heart."

Even when it was time for the clay class, the enthusiasm he had before had vanished, and when he took the clay, it was only to put it down again.

"I can't do anything good. I don't feel like doing it. *Sensei,* what could I make?"

I thought I had found a clue as to how I should talk with him.

"Well, then, shall I give you a problem? It's difficult. Is that all right?"

"It's okay, even if it's hard."

"Kiyoshi, what do you really want? You must have something you want, don't you?"

"What? I don't want anything. I want to die."

"If you have the strength to die, why don't you use it to stay alive?"

He must have thought I could see deep into his heart.

"Is it possible to express the feeling of wanting? For example, the desire for power, the desire for help. Try to express these feelings. You've got to listen to yourself quietly to know what you really want. In this case, the important thing is to express your desire not through things but to express them only through the movements of your body. Do you understand? When you suffer, you crouch. When you are happy, you spring up. Try to think this way. Man's feelings, you know, come out in his form."

I took his hands and showed him the body movements of happiness and sadness.

"I want that. I want this. Wow, this is difficult!"

"Sure it's hard to do, but I think you can do it."

"Well, I'll think about it."

Moving his head, his hands and all, he made various movements, but looking at his stiff motions, I wondered if it wasn't too difficult for him.

Then he made something in clay.

"*Sensei*, how about this?"

"Well, if it's a pauper begging, it's all right."

It was a work with only the hands outstretched.

One day toward the end of October he came to me again.

"How about this one?"

"You shouldn't try to think only with hand movements. Why don't you try to wish with your head, your hands and feet, with your whole body? That's what's important. It shouldn't take the appearance of receiving something but should be the feeling of need, of desire that emerges from within the body. For example, when you have a fever and want a glass of water, your hands reach out in a dynamic gesture and your mouth opens. If you have that feeling, you can naturally take that form."

"I guess I understand, though not clearly."

The poses of his clay figures began to show some movement, in the hands stretched forward and the head slightly inclined, but the mouth was not open wide enough nor the head slanted flexibly or far enough. Characteristics such as these are considered general tendencies in blind children's work.

At that point, I gave up thinking he could do any better.

By the middle of November, the sun was setting early and the mountains began to show that winter was approaching. Since the art classroom was now too cold a place to work with clay, eight students had to change to woodwork. That day Kiyoshi came to me as soon as the afternoon class began and pleaded.

"*Sensei*, let me work with the clay once more. I want to finish this without fail."

Since his homeroom with sunlight from the south was warmer than the art classroom, I suggested he work there.

Toward the end of the class period, I felt as though he were calling me so I went to his classroom.

Beyond the window glass was a very different person with the same profile, moving his hands wholeheartedly. When it appeared to me that the work was done, I went in the room, and just as I entered, he called me.

The sculpture bathed in the light of the setting sun expressed his burning desire. With the right hand extended forward and left hand on its chest, the figure somehow reminded me of the dignity of Buddhist sculpture. The gently inclined head turned up toward the sky with a look of despair and the open mouth crying out for something. The eyes were closed in sorrow. One foot a step forward of the other barely supported the whole body.

"Kiyoshi, this is it! It really is! This is very good. You finally did it."

"*Sensei*, really?"

"Yes, you really did it. You can make a wonderful work of art. This is something that you alone could create. Now please try hard to live again, all right?"

"Do you really understand how I feel?"

"Yes, I believe I understand. Yes, I do understand. I know very well how you must feel."

"*Sensei*, did you know all along?"

"Yes, I did. I heard your operation was a failure and I wanted to console you, but it would have been hypocritical since I can see. Kiyoshi, now I hope you can be as you were before."

"Yes."

"Now, how do you feel?"

"I can't give up hoping. I wonder if anyone can understand my feeling. I want eyes."

"Yes, that's true. Unfortunately nobody can truly understand."

The following spring a music box was sent to me from an acquaintance in Kyushu. When you opened the small black box, you could hear the lullaby of the Itsuki region. At noon recess, Kiyoshi came to the art classroom.

"*Sensei*, could I listen to the music box? I want one too."

"You want one, heh? Then shall we buy you one?"

"No, that would be too much for me to ask."

"Well, then if your work is selected for an exhibition, why don't I give you one as a present?"

"Oh, yes, that would make me happy. Then let me apply to this year's exhibition."

"Of course, and unless your work is accepted, I'll feel a lump in my throat. The music box is a good idea, isn't it. What tune do you like best?"

"I like "Akatonbo.*" I fell strong again. Wow, I'm happy, *Sensei*. Promise me, will you?"

I grasped his hand firmly.

"Let's try our best, let's try our best."

"All right."

*Publisher's note: "Red Dragonfly," a famous Japanese children's song.

The following November, the work entitled "I Want Eyes" was proudly accepted in the Nikaten Children's Art Exhibition. It made a deep impression upon its viewers. A film based on this story later received a Minister of State prize in a film festival.

Another New Task 1965

The sixteen years I have spent with the blind have passed by very quickly. During this time, many important changes have occurred within the school. The most significant development has been that the weak-sighted students have replaced the completely blind as the majority. The ratio of blind to weak-sighted children is now one to six. We are most pleased with this trend.

Because of this change, the question has arisen of whether or not the blind and the weak-sighted children should be taught in the same classes. The more education for the weak-sighted advances, the more it appears that the blind children might be left out.

Even with their very poor eyesight, weak-sighted children can read big printed letters as well as do brush drawing and calligraphy. When both the blind and the weak-sighted children study together, there is bound to be some discord between the two groups.

I happened to hear the following conversation between a blind child and a weak-sighted child in the sixth-grade class.

"How about this drawing? I did it. Isn't it good?"

"I want to draw too."

"It's impossible."

"Why? What if I draw one?"

"It would be just a mess. Because you can't see, you can't draw."

"What would happen if I did draw something anyway?"

"Then you would be able to stand on your own feet. You'd be a full person."

I worried about this sort of conversation, and began to wonder if the blind children might possibly be able to draw after all.

It seemed like such a crazy idea that probably no one had ever thought of trying to teach them. Was it clearly impossible?

I continued to ponder. To re-create the true essence of three-dimensional objects in two dimensions is possible only by using one's eyes. No matter how much I think about it, how I would go about it remains a puzzle. Only a being like God can foresee if such a thing is possible.

I knew that children who had lost their sight after the age of seven or eight could draw by relying on their memories of past experiences. But what about those who were born blind? Unless I could teach these children how to draw and effectively express their range of experience, I felt it would be impossible to say that the blind could also really draw.

I was most reluctant to undertake this risky venture. Events, however, developed in such a way that I could not avoid it.

In September of 1964, I started to teach the weak-sighted sixth-graders how to draw pictures with black ink and big brushes. They were enjoying this class no doubt because they could see the thick black lines very well. Then one blind girl quietly announced that she too would like to paint, the earnestness of her wish to join the others clearly evident in her voice.

I showed her how to hold the brush and just hoped she could do it. She drew a doll with a round head, a rectangular torso, and four straight line arms and legs.

Having thus arrived at the first step by accident, I decided to find out how the other blind children would approach drawing, and so I experimented by giving them all certain themes.

After seeing some of their attempts, I was ready to conclude that there were no similarities in the ways the blind and sighted people outlined the same objects. One child, for instance, expressed a teacup as two circles, one inside the other. The inner circle was the top rim of the cup, the outer the bottom rim. The results didn't seem promising.

Then in the drawings of two eighth-grade girls, I noticed something different. Each had her own way of drawing. For example, one girl had pictured a dog spread flat like an animal-skin rug, while another had painted a dog standing upright and readily recognizable by anyone.

I went on to study the other sample paintings of flowers, horses, dogs, fish, birds, and so forth, and realized that the blind students' paintings were on the whole slightly different from those of sighted children. Yet at the same time, I could say that they were clearly fine pictures. With this discovery I breathed a great sigh of relief.

In preparation for the day when they would take up brush drawing with the weak-sighted students as a regular class, I encouraged them to draw figures and forms in the air with their fingers.

On November 6, I decided to let the six blind students in elementary and junior high start their painting. So that they could understand the width of the lines they would be drawing, I shortened the tips of their brushes to spread just the width of their fingers.

They began practicing circles, triangles, and squares. Then each went on to develop his own techniques. The bigger their pictures, the more the parts scattered here and there on the page, and I soon discovered that large notebook paper was the best size for them to work with. They gradually mastered how much ink to use, how to guide the brush, and finally the correct posture.

Until graduation day that year, they enthusiastically practiced their drawing two hours every week. On March 5, they put down their brushes with eight perfect original paintings to their credit.

The weak-sighted children complimented them on their achievement.

"They do a good job, don't they?"

"They draw dynamically, and their lines don't tremble like ours. How do they do it?"

The blind children smiled and looked pleased.

"I like to paint now. It wasn't as difficult as I thought it would be."

"I never thought I could do it. But we can do a lot if we really try, can't we."

In the middle of April, the eight drawings were put together in a booklet entitled *Standing on Our Own Feet*, and copies were sent as gifts to institutes for the handicapped in seventy countries. It was widely reported in the foreign press and we received many letters of praise from France, Australia, New Zealand, and many other countries.

Among these complimentary letters, I received one critical note from a Japanese. It was easy to imagine that a lot of other people might also quietly hold this opinion. One portion of the letter said: "You have certainly succeeded in making these blind children paint pictures. However, they themselves cannot see their own work and sooner or later they will find emptiness in their efforts. There are many people who are still fine independent individuals even if they cannot draw. I think it's cruel to encourage them to draw what they cannot see."

Actually, there are several ways this particular problem can be handled. They best understand their pictures through their sensitive fingertips. The lines of a drawing can be traced in glue and then filled in with sand, or a dotted line made with a tracing wheel.

Having heard these children say, "I've always wanted to draw" and having even seen them draw linear pictures with Craypas, I can certainly now say that the blind also do draw even though they cannot see. I have interpreted this truth to mean that they draw for us who can see, to show us their world. No doubt if drawing were not a happy, easy experience for them, they wouldn't have taken up paint brushes in the first place.

Three years later we were all happily surprised when the writer of that particular letter wrote us again sending us words of encouragement and some records.

A Child Carrying Flowers, My Dog, Flowers, Motherbird and Babybird, A Horseman, My Wish, Mother and Me, Letting a Bird Free — looking at these India-ink paintings before her, one happy mother's eyes filled with tears and she said, "My child can draw. It is almost as though he were able to see. It is like the flower that blooms only once in three thousand years. To me, *Sensei* is like the buddha."

Thus, I have been able somehow to overcome my third task.

I have now spent nineteen years together with the blind children confronting and overcoming challenges, one after another.

What, I wonder, am I to do from this point on? Or rather, what should I do next?

The children will provide answers to these questions. So long as I continue my travel on this endless desert, I have no way of knowing where the next obstacle lies.

I shall most likely continue my travel alone, as before, filled with awe as I go.

2
Fish That Have Hands

Fundamental Shapes (first-grade boy)

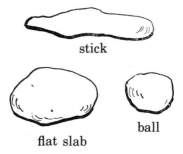

stick

flat slab

ball

The new first-graders usually get to know clay by pressing, patting, pounding, and pulling it apart. Some children sniff it, tear it into bits and throw it, or put it into their mouths. Others are afraid and will not even touch it.

Young children with normal ability generally take little bits of clay and first make them into sticks, flat slabs, and balls. They then combine these into more complex clay figures and objects. If the theme is fruit on a plate, for example, balls are placed on a flat slab.

The First Human Figure (first-grade girl)

man

As the children begin to experiment freely with the clay, they are surprised at the figures they can easily make. Their first clay shapes, for instance, are long, narrow sticks that are rolled with the palms of their hands. These sticks represent the human figure, usually Mother.

Such clay forms may look like only a human torso to most people, but a young blind child might easily call the same stick a trunk, a body, a chest, or a stomach, and so on.

Mother and I (first-grade girl)

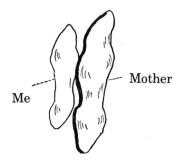

Me — — Mother

"Which one is Mother?"
"There! Naturally, the bigger one."
The outline of the girl herself in her mother's embrace is expressed by two sticks adhering to one another. Here again a person is just one stick of clay without arms or legs but now this child is using more than one figure in her compositions.

Flagpole Without a Flag (second-grade boy)

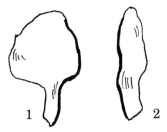

"What sort of thing is a national flag?"
"Gee, I don't know."
"In that case, do you know what a flag is?"
"Yes, I do. It's something everybody waves at athletic meets."
"I wonder what shape it has."
"It's something that flutters."

Because the appearance of thin cloth or paper is difficult for the blind to comprehend, they generally don't make the flags. Since the pole, however, is a sturdy thing that they can hold onto, they can be certain of its shape. They therefore end up making only the flagstaff. Illustration 1 has both a stick and a pennant which is represented by a flat slab and handle shape in clay. Illustration 2 is a flag with only the stick.

Person Holding a Flag (second-grade girl)

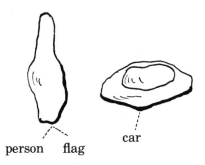

person   flag   car

"I wonder which is the flag."
"This is."
"Then, the person...."
"Here he is."

"They're the same thing, aren't they?"

"That's because the person is holding the flag."

To this child, both a flag and a person have the same stick shape. Therefore, he has combined them both into one unit. The car has no roof and no wheels, and there is a hole in it where the passengers get in. The person with the flag is waving goodbye to the people in the car.

Person Wearing Shoes (second-grade boy)

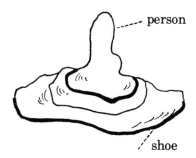

This is one example of the blind child's tendency in sculpture to make the parts he knows best the biggest. They are especially sensitive to things they can hold in their hands.

In this work, the boy knew a lot about shoes so he made the shoe bigger than the person wearing it. The form inside the shoe is the person's whole body; the head is where the body tapers off to a point. Another example, a piece showing "A Person Playing a Flute," was made with the flute bigger in size than the person playing it.

When this boy reached the sixth grade, he made a clay sculpture that was accepted in a public art exhibition.

A Person Seated at a Desk (first-grade boy)

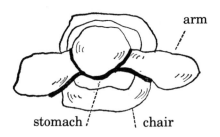

This creative little boy placed his "person" in a chair.

The round ball in this work is the head and big arms have been attached to it. The flat piece just underneath—the "stomach"—could also be called the torso. The flat piece below this represents the seat of the chair. The legs were too difficult to make, so they were left out. Attempting such a difficult pose indicated a big step in this child's artwork.

Piano (third-grade boy)

Blind children are most interested in the piano keyboard where the music originates.

The long narrow sticks here are the keys, not the piano wires. They were carefully created one by one and then stacked up to suggest that the piano has a great number of keys. The thick, flat piece below the keyboard is the piano's wooden case.

The Ship That Has Wheels (third-grade boy)

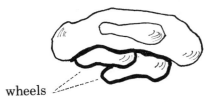

The vehicles the children usually make have large holes scooped out where people are supposed to get in. The one in this ship is in the middle. The two lumps beneath the ship are wheels. The artist put wheels on his boat because he knew cars and bicycles had them. Because these children don't know what transportation vehicles are really like even though they sit in them, they learn basic shapes like these from models and toys.

Airplane (fifth-grade girl)

The fuselage is like a shallow, broad-rimmed ashtray, and the sunken area is where people sit. There are no wheels or propellers.

This girl thinks that the wings of birds and of airplanes are very similar to a man's extended arms.

The School Bus (sixth-grade girl)

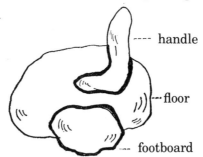

A very rare work, perhaps the best expression I have ever seen of a situation primarily understood and re-created through the sense of touch. Blind children cannot comprehend the size of their school bus.

"What is this little flat piece in front here?"

"It's what you step on when you get in."

"This pole?"

"What you hold as you are getting in."

"This big slab?"

"The floor of the bus."

The steps, the handrail, and the footboard were the parts she knew best from first-hand experience.

Mailbox With Feet (fourth-grade boy)

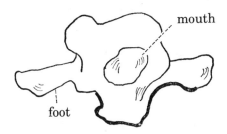

Letters written in braille are delivered without charge as a special service to the blind but this child didn't need to write letters so he had never used a mailbox.

"The hole in the middle is where you put them in, isn't it?" I asked him.

"Because it eats letters, I thought it should probably have a mouth."

"I wonder what these sticks are coming out the sides."

"Since it stands up all the time, it needs legs, doesn't it?"

This child's mailbox was a living creature.

Person (#1) (first-grade girl)

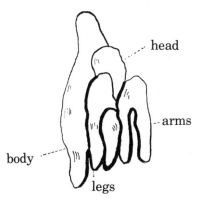

Very young blind children know their own bodies and those of models part by part but it is very difficult for them to imagine and create a whole body. The parts of this work—the torso, the legs, the head, and both the hands—were made piecemeal, and then put together.

The children repeat this same process when they make animals such as birds or dogs. Before long, however, they progress beyond this phase to building the basic skeletal structure of the whole body first and then refining it part by part.

Person (#2) (sixth-grade boy)

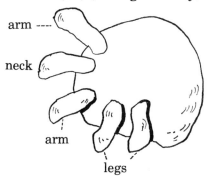

This artist is a child born without eyes. He finally reached the point where he included arms and legs on his work but he still didn't seem done. After careful thought, he added another stick of clay, the neck. A figure with a neck like this isn't seen very often.

This child said that the large disk in the center is the head, but it is actually the body. Before he could put the "head" in the right location, he took great pains trying it various ways.

Person (#3) (first-grade boy)

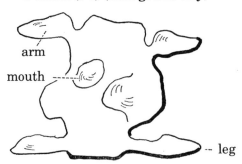

Although most blind children shape their early work as a collection of separate parts, the example shown here is an exception. This child shaped and drew out the figure's arms and legs from a single mass of clay. I call the former workers in clay, joiners, and the latter, casters.

First-graders tend to place the arms and legs in the parallel fashion pictured above. The raised portion in the center is the head and the open hole in front of it the mouth.

Before long, this little boy made the legs of his figures perpendicular to the torso. When he became a junior-high-school student, his work was accepted in the Nikaten Exhibition.

Person (#4) (third-grade boy)

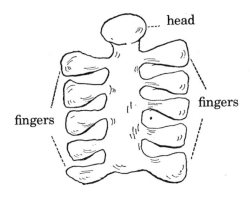

This figure is far from what sighted people would see as human, but it is, nonetheless, drawn from the model in this artist's mind.

The five narrow projections on each side of the torso are fingers of both hands. Often, in the second and third grades, children become intrigued with hands and like to make at least one large one to which they carefully attach the fingers.

Person (#5) (ninth-grade boy)

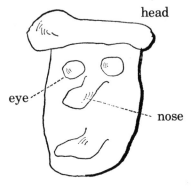

"This is a face, isn't it?"

"It's a person."

"Oh, I thought it was just a face."

"No, it shows the difference between a man and a face."

"I see, the eyes and the nose are below the head so the thing below that is the mouth, isn't it?"

"No, it's different."

"I wonder what it could be."

"Well, that's...that! Ha, ha, ha."

Face (#1) (fourth-grade girl)

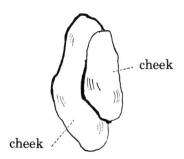

When one presses one's face with the palms of one's hands, the cheeks feel flat. This child thinks that the face is only two cheeks. In this example, the left and right cheeks, clay balls patted flat, were combined one on top of the other.

On complex surfaces such as the face with its nose and mouth, the children often cannot understand where the face begins or ends.

Face (#2) (fourth-grade girl)

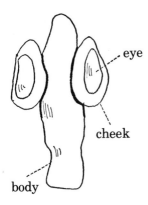

The face of this piece is two cheeks with balls of clay embedded for eyes. The stick in the middle is the torso, a familiar, archetypal human figure. The artist considered the eyes the most important feature of her work.

Face (#3) (eighth-grade girl)

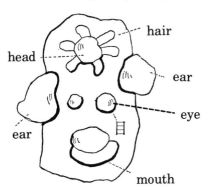

This piece is more advanced in composition. The head and face were fashioned separately. The little ball head, surrounded by strands of clay-roll hair, is depicted in a unusual way. In addition, the ears are flat and the lobes quite thin.

"You've done a fine job on the mouth."

"Did I? I made the lips like two pea-pods."

Of course, I thought to myself, "when I touch my lips, they do feel like two shelves!"

This face could probably be called a typical blind child's work.

Baby Fish (first-grade boy)

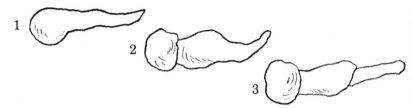

Just as they do human figures, my students make baby fish of clay sticks. Very often, however, the fish's basic stick shape differs in its swollen head and tapered tail.

After making his first, simple fish, this little boy went on to make a second one. He attached a sphere-shaped head and molded the body into two parts. He then made a fish with a head, a trunk, and a tail. Having taken three such basic steps, he next began to concentrate on details—the eyes, the scales, and the split rear fin.

Fish (#1) (fifth-grade girl)

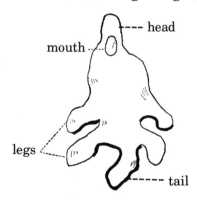

This fish has a pointed snout for poking and a slit for breathing. There are two narrow projections on each side where the dorsal and pectoral fins should be. These could also be considered as corresponding to arms and legs.

The young artist says the rear fin of her fish is what the fish "wags," probably because she thinks it is like a dog's tail.

Fish (#2) (second-grade boy)

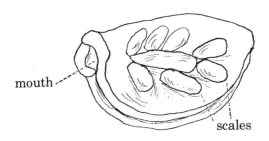

If one looks carefully at the abdomen of this fish, one will notice that the child folded a sheet of clay in two, cupping it so as to leave the inside hollow and the pointed end open to make the mouth. The only piece I have ever seen with such an inside cavity, his fish looks much like a fortune cookie. The clay fragments represent the fish's big scales.

Fish (#3) (sixth-grade girl)

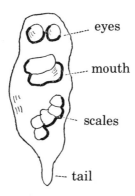

The eyes of this fish look like those in a human face. Two

overlapping disks—the lips—indicate the mouth. The five attached flat pieces are the scales. They have a rough texture which appeals to one's sense of touch and suggests that the artist had touched fish.

This child also seems to have thought a fish's tail was just like a dog's.

Crab (#1) (eighth-grade girl)

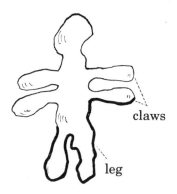

claws

leg

The students learn the painful way when they reach out to touch a thing and are pinched in the process. Afterward, however, they are quick to imagine what that animal must be like. Unless the blind child has a great deal of courage and trust in sighted people, he cannot rely on his imaginative powers to make things.

Here the right and left claws, resembling a pair of scissors, are positioned where a person's arms would normally be. This girl seems to have created the head and legs from her previous experience making human models.

Crab (#2) (fourth-grade boy)

----- eight legs

When I ask my students how many legs a crab has, many of them say it has four legs shaped like those of a dog. These children have never touched a crab's legs and are unable to place the crab's feet or even shape them.

Accordingly, because the crab is a marine animal, they shape it like a fish and attach the legs like dog's legs, and an imaginary crab is born.

Crab (#3) (sixth-grade boy)

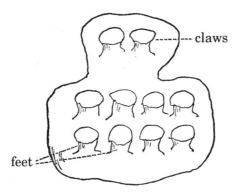

This little boy says the two rows of stump-like projections are the crab's eight legs. He also says the two projections above, in the part looking like the head, are not the eyes but the claws. His knowledge and conception of a crab's feet and claws make this an unusual work. I find it interesting that this crab also is based on a human model.

Butterfly (eighth-grade girl)

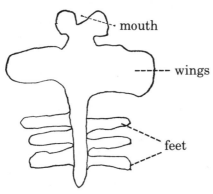

I first thought this work was an airplane. Although the students all know airplanes through toys, they don't know much about butterflies. Therefore, this child modeled her butterfly's wings on those of a toy plane. Because both fly, she must have thought they would resemble one another.

The pronged head is the mouth and the six extensions on the thorax are the legs.

There are very few examples of butterflies in my blind children's artwork.

Dog (#1) (first-grade boy)

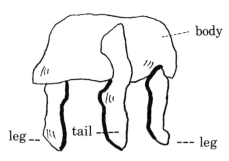

Because blind children often find dogs frightening, many will not pat them. And even when they touch toy dogs, they won't make the head because they find it too complicated to re-create.

It was difficult for this little boy to put all four legs on his dog, so he attached two as though they were a person's legs. As with many beginning dog figures, the tail is more familiar to the artist than the head. Therefore, deeming it a very important part of the dog, he put a big fat one right in the center as the finishing touch.

Dog (#2) (fourth-grade girl)

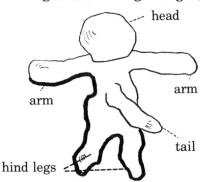

This artist was even afraid to touch stuffed and toy animals, so everyone called her "scaredy cat." After spending a long time tracing outlines of dogs in the air, she made her dog. His front legs, which she called "arms," were like a person's outstretched arms. She made the tail with a thick stick and put it right on the middle of the back. The head was difficult for her so she made a sphere and left it at that.

Dog (#3) (third-grade boy)

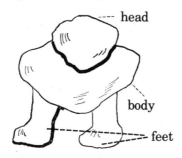

Even though this child had a dog at home to pat, he said he didn't understand its form very well. When people see a dog, they understand its shape right away. However, it isn't a shape that one can quickly comprehend when one depends on the sense of touch.

This piece is composed of a triangular body, a round head, and a front and a hind leg. The artist, a clever and sensitive child, knew that a dog had four legs. Three months later he made his dog's head oblong, and included a tail and all four legs.

Bird (#1) (seventh-grade girl)

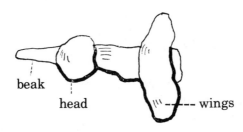

With birds, the fluffy feeling of feathers makes many blind

children uneasy. Although they don't like to touch stuffed birds, they do have a good understanding of a bird's bill and wings. This bird, like so many others, has a stick body, a round head, and flat wings. When it came to the legs, however, the artist didn't know what shape to make them or where to put them.

Bird (#2) (fourth-grade girl)

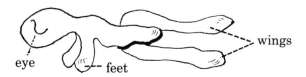

This bird is unique, with its flat, double-layered wings. The eyes are indicated by hollows on either side of the head.

"When he flies, his back wings flap back and forth just as you do when you clap your hands."

The artist was especially interested in wings, and after careful thinking about their function, she made this work.

Chicken (#1) (fourth-grade girl)

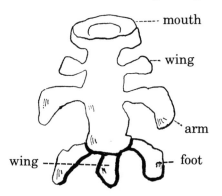

This little girl says the mouth of her chicken is shaped like a bugle because when it eats grain, it must open its mouth very wide.

"I wonder if birds have arms," I said.

"Well, people have them, don't they?"

She was probably thinking of a human body when she put long arms between the wings and the legs. The varying lengths of the arms, legs, and wings show how well this child understands chickens.

Chicken (#2) (fourth-grade girl)

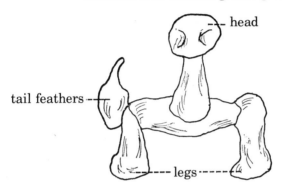

The pole-like body of this chicken is unusual because it is supported by legs at both ends. The neck rises from the middle to hold the ball-shaped head, and the hollows of the eyes represent the face. The tail feathers attached above one leg are another unusual feature.

House (#1) (third-grade boy)

Many of the houses the blind children make have no roof, only walls in which windows and doors are sometimes scooped out or added separately.

Here a ball has been placed on a flat slab of clay which is not the floor but the *tatami**. The round object in the center is the artist himself.

*Publisher's note: *Tatami* are thick, tightly woven straw mats that cover the floorboards of many Japanese homes.

"Where is the roof?"

"I haven't touched it so I don't know."

One can imagine how important the process of learning by touch is. When, how, and the order in which to touch things can be terribly significant in a blind child's perception of things around him.

House (#2) (fourth-grade boy)

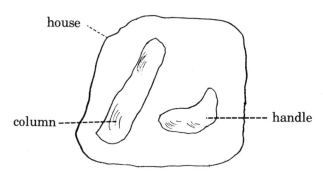

This is just two clay sticks placed on top of a clay slab but to this boy it represents a house. The stick at the left is the house's main support column; the curved piece at the right is the main door handle. The rectangular slab at the bottom shows that the boy thought of the house as a box with the floor its bottom. A roof has no place in his scheme.

With such works, the viewer must ask the designer for an explanation, since only parts of the whole are included.

The Doghouse (second-grade boy)

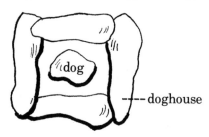

In this example, the dog sleeps in the middle of his doghouse, represented by the stick enclosure. (When blind children paint, they picture a house as a rectangle in the same way.) The dog, a lump without legs or head, is the first one a child makes.

In order to make three-dimensional objects such as houses, the children have two principal methods of presenting their ideas. One way is to take a lump of clay and hollow out from it a hole with a flat bottom, and the other is to represent it as only a flat surface and outlines, as in this example.

Bird in a Tree (second-grade boy)

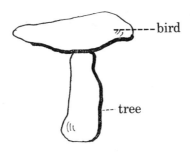

This is not a hammer! It is a bird that has landed in a tree. It is an elementary stick-figure bird, and so it has no wings and no feet.

When two shapes are combined, arranging them parallel or one on top of the other is easy. T-shaped combinations, however, are difficult.

Man on a Horse (second-grade boy)

This piece is merely a combination of two prototype figures, a man and a horse. The person is riding the horse, however, and that is a very difficult subject to express.

Even though I try to encourage the students to imitate the

posture of horse and rider, there are many who do not succeed in making the rider perpendicular to the horse's back.

A Youth Catching Insects (seventh-grade boy)

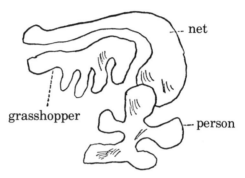

net

grasshopper

person

This composition consists of three pieces. The four-legged thing at the left is the grasshopper. The person on the right is a child. The long stick above the two is the net. The little boy is holding out the net to catch the grasshopper. The insect, the biggest figure in the picture, shows where the artist's main interest lies. What the artist calls the net here is only a pole without the netting to the viewer.

Pitcher (fourth-grade boy)

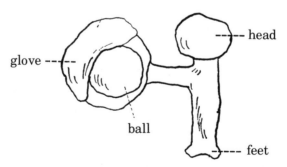

glove

head

ball

feet

This work is a good illustration of how blind children conceive of the relative size of parts in a composition. Because the ball in the glove is the biggest part, for instance, it is clearly the artist's special area of interest. In contrast, he worries surprisingly little about how the pitcher himself is presented. This human figure has only one arm and the legs are indicated by only a little modeling at the bottom. The blind artist's completed picture differs greatly in conception from those of most artists.

Monster (#1) (fourth-grade boy)

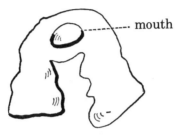

"Hey, *Sensei*, what do you think this is? It's a monster. Aren't you afraid?"

My student says the gaping mouth in the center is so big it can eat people. He can't overcome his preconception that all monsters are basically humanoid. Even when students make the gods or the sun, they often portray them as human figures.

This work shows that blind students can also create fictitious and invisible beings.

Monster (#2)   (sixth-grade boy)

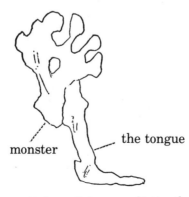

This is a monster so it doesn't have a distinctly recognizable shape.

The part that looks like fingers might be viewed as the monster's face; the hole in the center could be either an eye or a mouth. The four extensions of the head may be either feelers or tentacles. The long dangling thing below the face is the tongue. The boy made the tongue long to surprise people with it.

Ghost (fourth-grade boy)

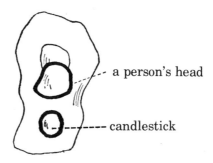

a person's head

candlestick

"If dead people come to visit, they're ghosts, aren't they?"
"Yes, that's right."
"This is how it looks if a dead person comes up out of the grave. You can see his head has already come out. It's scary, isn't it?"
The round object in the middle is a person's head.

The Sea   (fourth-grade girl)

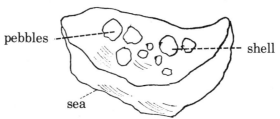

pebbles

shell

sea

Even though this work is said to be the sea, the viewer will find few traces of what he would expect in a seascape.

In order to indicate where the water was in her artwork, the girl made her sea like a deep tray, the center of which was supposedly filled with water. She says the oceans are the puddles of the earth. The small fragments in the center are pebbles and shells. It is a composition with a lyrical flavor, probably inspired by her experience on a shell-gathering expedition.

3
A World Without Light

Shell Gathering (fourth grade)

My class and I planned a trip to the seashore to gather shells at low tide. I meant to teach the students a little about it beforehand, but I was taught instead.

"What kinds of shells can you find on the beach?" I asked.

One boy answered, "Clams and mussels."

"How do you tell them apart?"

The same boy replied, "Clam shells are smooth, mussels are rough."

"You know a lot about them, don't you. Now let's make big forks to gather them with," I instructed.

"We don't need them," another boy explained. "If we use them, we can't tell which shells are which. Hands are the best tool. We know what we have as soon as we touch it."

"I'm sorry, how silly," I said.

A third child commented, "Teachers don't understand things at all, even though they can see."

Sighted people distinguish shells by color and design, but these children relied on their ability to distinguish different surfaces. If they used a fork, it would take longer to separate the shells from the stones.

Last Trip to our Favorite Seashore (third grade)

We went to the same seashore every year but this time would be our last since the area was planned for construction. What were the children's impressions of this place they had so often explored at low tide?

"*Sensei*, whenever we gather shells, there is only a little water in the sea. Nature makes it very convenient for us, doesn't it?"

The Giraffe (third grade)

Forty primary-school children went to a city zoo for their spring excursion. Because the elephants, monkeys, and other animals were all in cages, making it impossible to touch them, the children experienced only the occasional screeches of monkeys.

"Why are giraffes and elephants put in cages? Poor animals," asked one young girl.

"You have to touch to know them, don't you?" I said.

"Yes, I'd like to touch them."

"I wonder how big a giraffe is," I said, as though I didn't know.

"Oh, probably about the size of a dog," another girl suggested.

Some people are critical and wonder why we take the children to zoos since they cannot touch the animals. It is hard to know how to answer.

Beforehand, at school, we encourage them to touch toy animals and make their own versions in clay. Then, at the zoo, they try to imagine the animals by their smells and noises. Their impressions, however, are far removed from the real animals. The size of each animal is particularly hard for them to grasp. Many of them think giraffes and elephants are just the width of their arm span.

A Voice Beauty (sixth grade)

One day, a sixth-grade girl transferred from another primary school to our school.

Quite a few children come to schools like ours when they discover poor eyesight is the reason they are falling behind in class. Soon after coming, they start doing better in class and become more cheerful.

A blind boy was the first person to speak with this new girl.

"As soon as I heard your voice, I liked it. Since you have a beautiful voice, you must be beautiful too. Let's sit together on the school bus this afternoon. I feel happier now."

Blind children can imagine the age, build, and state of a person's mind by hearing how that person talks. Sometimes our students surprise us teachers by accurately judging how we are feeling.

When talking to a blind person, it's important to tell him who you are, and speak in a friendly and polite manner, looking him in the face. To the blind, people with fine voices and smooth skin are beautiful. They also intuitively seem to know if a person's soul is beautiful.

Fresh Air (seventh grade)

One day we climbed a hill — an historical battle field — behind the school. Because clay oozes out of the ground there, the children call it clay mountain.

When we reached the top, I could see the city of Kobe spread out like a fan. Two blind students had different impressions.

"Everywhere we stop seems just the same to me, however high we climb."

"Isn't this mountain pretty low? When I climbed a high mountain before, it seemed as though fresh air was continually whooshing up from below."

The sighted determine the height of a mountain by the scenery they see. The blind, however, can tell the altitude by the difference in the air they breathe and by the cool breezes they feel at the summit.

Rainy Days-off (eighth grade)

One day it rained all morning.

With his new shoes soaking wet, Tokio came into the room complaining.

"The wind blew so strongly I couldn't find my way to school. My sense of intuition didn't work and I fell in a ditch. I couldn't hold my umbrella against the wind, and the cars splashed mud all over me. I really hate rainy days like today."

"I know what you mean. Why doesn't our school make a rule that we don't come on rainy days? Then we'd all be happy. Why don't the teachers understand this?"

It is said that blind people can tell direction by feeling air currents. On rainy or windy days, those currents become irregular. Umbrellas also make it difficult for them to distinguish among all the noises they hear.

The Shade   (sixth grade)

Strong rays of the summer sun have been shining on the school ground since morning, and the buildings' shadows revolve on the ground like a sundial.

Two blind and one weak-sighted boy are playing with a ball. The weak-sighted child can hardly stand the strong light.

"The sun is too bright. I can't keep my eyes open. Let's play in the shade."

"What's shade?" inquired one blind boy.

"Oh, don't you know? It means under a roof," replied the other.

The blind boy has learned what shade is from a sighted person; somebody might have explained it to him thus. Here he really meant that they should play in the shadow of the school building. There are quite a few examples like this when the blind have their way of interpreting the words of sighted people.

Braille   (ninth grade)

The dots used in braille are tiny. One can read them directly with one's eyes, although it is very tiring to do so. It is amazing that blind grade-school children can read braille at the same speed as a normal rate of speaking.

A forty-year old man who had lost his sight rather late in life told me, "I have somehow managed to learn to write braille but I still have a great deal of trouble reading it. I suppose the older you get, the less sensitive your fingers become. It is very frustrating to find that my fingers are not good enough for reading. I tell you frankly it's driven me to tears at times."

A child commented about braille: "I have been reading braille since the first grade but it is especially difficult to read in very cold and very warm weather. When it's hot, my fingers perspire. Long novels in braille soon wear me out. Reading braille is exhausting work."

Braille was invented in 1829 by Louis Braille, a teacher of the blind in Paris. In 1891, Kuraji Ishikawa, a teacher of the blind in Tokyo, adapted it to the Japanese language.

Three Frightening Things (third grade)

In Japan, there is a saying that the three most dangerous and frightening things are earthquakes, thunder, and fires. For Toshio, a blind boy, the list is rather different. His list represents three major fears of most blind people.

"Three things I really fear are hit-and-run drivers, mice, and puddles. Can you guess why?"

Once a car grazed him and knocked his white cane away. Another time some mice ran around his house while he was alone at home. Once he stepped into a deep puddle on a rainy day while taking his normal route to school through a construction site. All three of his fears are based on actual frustrating experiences for which he can blame no one.

The Star Festival* (fourth grade)

On the day of the Star Festival, the children wrote down their wishes on strips of paper and attached them to colorful streamers. Some read "Oh stars, give me eyes" in braille.

Haruji was called "Professor" by the other children since he knew a lot about many things. When he announced he was going to make a copy of the Milky Way out of clay, I put some rather rough questions to him.

*Publisher's note: The Star Festival is a traditional event held in the summer on July 7th. It is based on a legend about two stars who are lovers. For a misdeed, they were sent to opposite ends of the Milky Way and can only meet once a year when their paths come near each other. On that day, Japanese children make wishes and fix them to gay streamers and bamboo branches.

"Where is the Milky Way?" I asked.
"It's above, in the sky."
"What is the sky?"
"The sky is in the firmament where the stars are."
"What are the stars?"
"They are what shine in the sky."
"What does shine mean?"
"Oh, I don't know that."

Physical Checkup (sixth grade)

At the beginning of second semester, the children all have their height and weight checked. Afterward, a boy with one good eye came into the craft classroom, laughing so hard he was holding his sides.

"It was so funny. A teacher told us to get undressed so Fujio took off everything, his underpants included! Ha ha ha, ha ha ha!"

Fujio protested. "But to get undressed means that you become naked. Well, anyway, the teacher's words were inaccurate to begin with."

Fujio was born blind. When sighted children are told to undress, they hesitate. This boy, however, with no such inhibitions, took his teacher's words literally.

The Sun Flag (The Japanese National Flag) (third grade)

Our school was to go to a nearby street to welcome the Torchbearers who ran to Tokyo for the Olympic games. Each child had been given a red and white paper flag.

Senji felt the surface of his flag very carefully.

"I've always wondered what the Sun Flag was really like, but it's just an ordinary sheet of paper attached to a bamboo stick."

Even though there were red circles printed on the flags, the students couldn't feel them, and some of them thought the Sun Flag was really only the red outline of a circle on a white background.

Composition on a School Excursion (sixth grade)

For the annual fall school excursion, the teachers always plan a hiking course that will strengthen the children's legs. Walking through pine tree forests and climbing up slopes, however, is mentally as well as physically exhausting for them.

Guided by a girl's helping hand, Shuichi had just reached the top of a steep slope, and he sat down to rest.

"Hmm, that was a long, hard walk. Tomorrow our teacher will probably have us write something about this excursion. I will write that it was rough going. I wonder if the teacher will get mad."

Riding buses and trains, chattering, and eating picnic lunches are the parts of school excursions the children like the best. When we take them to visit the ancient capitals of Nara and Kyoto, they find the temples beyond their comprehension. For the same reason, trips to the aquarium or the science museum are also boring. The teachers also find it very difficult to explain what their pupils cannot touch.

Mother's Handkerchief (fourth grade)

After the fall athletic meet, winter began to approach, and a quiet atmosphere settled over the school.

Etsuji, who didn't attend gym class, came into the craft classroom.

"I haven't seen your mother around the school recently," I remarked.

"She's been in bed ill," he replied.

"I'm sorry to hear that."

He took a small, soiled handkerchief from his pocket.

"*Sensei*, this is Mother's smell. Smell it."

The handkerchief smelled of Cresol, an antiseptic solution. His mother works as a hospital attendant. Usually he comes to school hand in hand with his mother every morning, but today he had the smell of Cresol to remind him of his mother.

Wire Netting (fourth grade)

Today, December 10, the classroom temperature fell below

50°F. and we turned on the heating. When it's cold, it makes reading braille much more difficult, so good heating is essential.

When I entered the classroom, Isamu called out to me. He sounded as though he had discovered something mysterious.

Sensei, will you come here and take a look at this. There are holes in here."

"Where? If there are, then we've got to do something."

He took my hand and led me to a far corner of the room. Then he put my fingers through the open spaces of a wire screen surrounding the stove which keeps the children from burning themselves.

This boy's observation is a perfect example of the differences in perceptions of sighted people and those of the blind.

The sighted really consider wire netting to be only the wire itself. The blind, on the contrary, consider wire netting to be only the spaces among the wires. For them, the screen is nothing but a series of holes.

A Winter Morning (ninth grade)

At the end of a long, quiet corridor, I heard a coin drop. Then a high-pitched girl's voice called out.

"Excuse me! Will somebody come here and lend me an eye!"

I heard footsteps running in that direction.

The blind can handle problems like this by themselves when the things they drop don't roll. But with coins, they become helpless. With the help of those who went to this girl's aid, she found her coin again.

Vinyl Tape (fifth grade)

One evening in February we had snow in Kobe, a rather rare event. The following day it was about two inches deep. The children ran about, throwing snowballs and thoroughly enjoying themselves. When the bell rang, they were not happy to come inside.

I heard a blind girl say to a friend, "Oh, my fingertips feel just as if I had vinyl tape on them. I can't read braille like this. What should I do?"

A Water Pillow* (second grade)

There was a flu epidemic going around, and we began to notice many absences at school.

One girl who had been absent was back so I asked her how she was.

"When I stay in bed, I get scared of the water pillow so I'd rather be at school."

"Why are you afraid of it?"

"Because it moves around as if it were alive, and I get scared."

The After-Graduation Party (advanced class)

Several days after commencement exercises for our high-school students and the advanced class, we had a graduation party.

Many girls get their hair permanent-waved soon after commencement apparently because it is advantageous to look older if one is going to be a masseuse.

"Your hair looks nice. Can you tell how it looks? It's nicely done, really," I told one former student.

"Well, probably this is what the beautician thought was right for me. Somehow when I touch it, though, I don't like it. Of course I have no way of looking at it in a mirror. If you can tell with your eyes that I look nice, then I feel satisfied. That makes me feel good."

Blind girls also put on their own makeup but sometimes they don't know how to use it effectively so that they end up with too much rouge, for instance. This is one thing we should teach them at school.

A Toy Dog (second grade)

Masami always made his clay models of dogs look like human figures so I bought him a toy dog. He spent a lot of time examining it and seemed especially interested in its legs.

"Oh, now I get it! Dogs walk in sleeping position, on their stomachs.

*Publisher's note: Similar to a hot-water bottle, a water pillow is made of thick rubber. It is filled with cold water or ice and is used as a pillow to lower a fever.

This child thought dogs walked on two feet, as humans do. When he discovered the toy dog had four legs, he concluded that they take the same position walking as a man lying on his stomach when he's sleeping.

The Colors of Clay (seventh grade)

The pliancy of the clay students like to work with seems to differ according to age. Elementary-school children like to work with soft clay while junior-high students prefer harder clay.

The two clay colors we use are brick and gray.

Taro had just taken some clay from the bottom of the supply jar.

"*Sensei*, today's clay feels soft and sticky so I'm sure I know its color," he exclaimed proudly.

Some have tried to teach the blind colors by associating them with the senses. They explain white, for instance, as being cold like snow or red as hot like fire. Such knowledge often turns out to be useless or creates misunderstanding. For example, blind children sometimes make the mistake of thinking a certain color is synonymous with a certain texture.

Because this boy was born without eyes he associated the degree of the clay's pliability, which he knew, with the clay's color, which he had only heard sighted people talk about.

A Bird as Model (third grade)

On Animal Day, the Kobe society for the prevention of cruelty to animals gave the children a bird in a cage. Afterwards, they spent many hours listening to it sing.

"Let's take it out of the cage and set it free."

"I wonder if it will let us touch it."

"I want to make its shape in clay."

"Do you know how birds are shaped? Do you want to touch a stuffed bird?" I asked.

"I know its shape so I don't need to touch a stuffed one. I have a picture of a model bird in my head."

Up to the third grade, the students never try to copy actual objects even when I let them touch them. "I can easily imagine what that model bird is like," the child is saying to himself. "I know a bird has a round head, a long body, and flat wings." Thinking this, he would make his clay figure by taking a ball and attaching it onto a roll to make the head and the body. Then he would attach two flat pieces as wings on the back, which is further down the roll.

For most young children, legs are too difficult to make.

Once I asked a twelve-year-old blind child about various shapes.

"Do you know what an organ is? What shape does it have?"

"It's square. The front is like stairs."

"What about the shape of a spoon?"

"The tip is round and smooth. The part you hold is a long stick."

"What about a teapot?"

"It's round and smooth. It has a hole at the mouth where you can stick your finger."

"A dog?"

"I'm afraid of dogs because they bite."

"A human face?"

"The head is round and the face is flat."

"A fish?"

"A fish has a round head and a long tail. I haven't seen the feet yet."

The Smell of Clay (ninth grade)

The clay crock in the workroom is big enough for a child to get in. For quite a while, Tokio had stood quietly with his head inside the jar but since it was time to take out the clay, I went to ask him what he was doing.

"Did you get stuck in the jar?"

"*Sensei*, could you please be quiet for a minute?"

"What's going on?"

"*Sensei*, this clay smells like a house. Why?"

For Tokio, the smell of a house is the smell of fresh plaster. For people who see, this is only the smell of new walls. I had carelessly not noticed it before.

Four-legged Rooster (seventh grade)

First period I have no class so that is when I prepare the students' work for firing. One morning a girl came looking for me.

"*Sensei*, are you there?"

"Yes."

"*Sensei*, do you still have the bird I made yesterday? If you do, please break it."

"Why, when you made it so carefully?"

"Mother told me that chickens have two legs. When I told her mine had four, she said my work must be very strange. So, please break it, will you?"

The rooster she made had four legs and two spurs.

This girl is blind from birth but why had such a misunderstanding occurred to someone so smart as to include spurs on her rooster? Through works such as this, I can understand how these children "see" the world.

Details (third grade)

Because blind children's work takes simple forms, it generally has the feeling of abstract art. For this reason too, one figure tends to look like another. I teach them to overcome this by encouraging them to stress details.

"Your works are so vague and simple. The sixth-graders' efforts don't differ much from those of the second-graders. So today in class, let's use each other as live models and search out the striking, detailed aspects of your subject — nostrils, toes, and so forth."

"Ahem, *Sensei*, do you mean *every* thing?" one boy asked shyly.
"Well, not always *every* thing."

Graduation Mementos (ninth grade)

I fired the children's artwork to make them mementos for graduation.

"As my graduation present to you all, I'd like you each to take home your artwork. Take whatever you like," I told them.

"*Sensei*, I want a good one since it will be a memento for the rest of my life," one child told me.

"What would you like?"

"A smooth one."

For the blind, beautiful means smooth and nice to touch. He took home the piece I gave him and put it in a very special place in his house.

A Wooden Box (fourth grade)

In order to teach the children the difference between flat objects and cubic objects, I showed them a wooden box, ten feet square, without a lid. Katsuji felt the inside and the outside carefully. Then with his palm still inside the box, he asked me, "*Sensei*, is this the inside or the outside? I have been touching it too long; now I am confused."

Unless there is a clear difference between the feel of the outside and the inside, a blind child finds it hard to tell which is which. This box was too big for them. They would have understood better if they could have encircled it with their hands.

A Red Craypas (sixth grade)

One girl who had recently lost her sight drew a picture with Craypas. It was about young children playing in the schoolyard, and was well done and readily understood by everyone.

"How did you draw this?" I asked her.

"Someone would say, 'Lend me a red Craypas,' and she would take it from my box. When she returned it, I would tell myself,

'This is a red Craypas,' and put it aside at the edge of the box. When I had fixed every color like this, I no longer needed to ask anyone every time I wanted a certain color. The ones who have borrowed Craypas from me are happy and so am I because I keep track of the colors. It works out well.

"I can still remember the colors and shapes of objects, and I use my fingers to keep the lines from overlapping when I do complicated parts. If you had to give up painting just because you'd become blind, you would feel resentful, wouldn't you? Most important, you'd feel ashamed in front of children who can see."

Before this girl lost her sight, her paintings were quite realistic. After she lost her sight, however, she began to draw diagram-like pictures of the sort a sighted first-grader usually makes. She says she still remembers colors and shapes but they are gradually fading from memory. I suppose other blind painters and sculptors face the same problems.

The Three-View Mirror (sixth grade)

Several little girls were conferring. They had decided to make a dressing table and mirror of cardboard. I asked them what they thought a mirror was like.

"It's to see your face," one weak-sighted child answered.

"But you can understand your own face just by touching it," protested a blind girl.

The weak-sighted girl explained, "The mirror is what tells you whether your face is pretty or not without your touching it. Sighted people use it."

"Then what about my face? Tell me if I'm pretty or not."

"*Sensei*, how about me?" Toshiko, another blind girl, asked me.

"You're very pretty. You are all pretty like goddesses. Yes, Toshiko, yes, Hiroko, you too!"

"Wow, I'm happy," said Toshiko.

"Hmm, really?" said Hiroko thoughtfully. "*Sensei*, I want to ask a question so please don't get mad, okay?"

"I won't. What is it you want to ask me?"

"Can you really see, *Sensei*?"

"What is it like to see?" asked another blind girl.

I hesitate to try to tell them what seeing is. I don't want to suggest that I might be more fortunate than they are.

A Saw (sixth grade)

The children are very fond of doing woodwork with saws and hammers. Before they start, I always warn them to use tools carefully for I understand from my experiences that they have a very narrow focus of attention.

"Listen, everyone, this is a saw. You use the zigzag edge to cut through wood. Has anybody here ever used a saw before?"

One blind student had. "Once I sawed some wood at home. While I was doing it, my older brother came running up to me, yelling, 'Hey, stop, stop it! Now you're cutting a corner pole of the house. What if it falls down?' "

"Oh, darn, it would have been funny if it had!" grinned another blind boy mischievously.

To See with Hands (fourth grade)

Sometimes blind children also use the word "see." A number of people have asked me why. Of course they use it in a different way.

"When I say that I 'see,' I could really say that my hands see. They are very inquisitive. They never stop touching, exploring, seeing, so I can know the world, whether it be a human face or a snake or a lion."

The verb "to see" refers not only to the capacity for using one's eyes. It also means the ability to use one's other senses to determine what things are.

An Audible Dream (fifth grade)

"Recently my dead grandma keeps coming to me in dreams. I wonder why?" I overheard one girl tell her friends.

"What does she do in the dreams?" I couldn't resist asking her.

"Well, last time she kept putting a sheet of paper in her wallet and then taking it out again as though it were money. Then she handed me the paper and told me, 'Keep it carefully 'cause you can't do anything without money.'

"Since my grandma was very money-conscious, I'm worried that they haven't let her into heaven yet."

"How did she look in your dreams?" I asked her.

"*Sensei*, our dreams are like radios, so to speak."

Blind people have dreams based primarily on words, sounds, and textures. I have heard them describe dreams about forgetting schoolbags, fires, worms, getting lost, getting run over by cars, and deceased parents.

Particularly unusual was a dream one child remembered in which he felt the roughness of a scrubbling brush.

A Building Just for Us (seventh grade)

The afternoon class had just started.

"Ken-chan isn't here yet. I wonder what happened," said one weak-sighted boy.

"He was crying in the washroom," said another.

"He must have hit himself on one of the pillars in the corridor. Poor Ken-chan," a third said.

"This school building is so clumsily built that I can't keep track of the number of times I hit myself in one day," stated the only completely blind boy present.

"You are the clumsy one," said the first.

"When you are small and still inexperienced, you hit yourself so many times that by the time you are an adult, you have become an expert at avoiding obstacles."

"Yes, but in the meantime, isn't it pretty rough on you? Your faces end up all knocked out of shape," commented another weak-sighted child warmly.

"I really wish they'd make a special building for us," the completely blind boy concluded. He had obviously thought very carefully about this problem.

Quite a few of the children have scars and bumps on their faces and hands.

I very rarely hear of schools anywhere that are especially designed and equipped for the blind. Even though teachers at schools for the blind sometimes discuss the possibility of constructing special buildings, at the present time they usually decide on the less expensive course of helping the blind adjust to ordinary buildings.

The Magnifying Glass (sixth grade)

Some weak-sighted children use big magnifying glasses to read books and look at small things such as insects. For blind children, the feel of the smooth curved glass is itself a wonder.

"What is this smooth thing used for?" a blind child asked a weak-sighted child.

"It's a glass for things like seeing insects," he explained.

"Oh, you mean that the insects wear glasses?"

"No, silly, small things like insects appear large through this glass."

"Then, what happens to big things?"

"Gee, it's tiring. You don't know anything."

"Just because you can see a little, you think you're really a big person, don't you?"

An Air Box (ninth grade)

Visitors to our school are often amazed that small children walk smoothly and rapidly through the corridors and the classrooms. I have asked the children how they do it but they seem to have trouble expressing their own world in words.

"What do you feel when you are walking down a corridor?" I asked one blind boy.

"When I walk in the center of a corridor, I feel the air on both sides of my body as if it were supporting me. If the air seems to stop moving around me, I know I've come to a corner. For me, the school building is like a box filled with air."

This is the finest explanation I've ever heard to my question. It is perhaps easier to understand if you think of the corridor as an engine cylinder and the blind person as a piston.

Because the blind can tell where they are and where they are going by the movement of air against their foreheads, sometimes they bump into obstacles below their waists.

Walking Outside (eighth grade)

Since we have our own school bus, only a few students use canes and walk to school. I asked these few how they manage to leave their homes and go places by themselves.

A blind girl had the following explanations.

"The center of the road is easy to tell because the ground swells slightly. The sides of the road smell like ditches and drainage water. At the crossroads, different sounds and smells come from each direction so I can decide which way to go. I know how long a road is or how it connects to another by its unevenness. When I come to a high wall or a building blocking my way, I somehow sense its heaviness and naturally come to a stop."

Another child added his ideas.

"When you hear a car approaching, you shouldn't hurry to the side of the road. Instead, you should go to the center and raise your cane. This turns out to be much safer. It may sound as though we are taking advantage of the fact that we're blind but we have no choice. Once we step out of our homes or the school, we always risk getting killed."

"Even though I might walk into many things, how I wish I could walk freely to far-away places. But everybody worries about me so much," sighed another.

According to Japanese traffic law, the blind must always walk with a white cane and drivers should slow down or stop when they see it.

A Red Dress (fourth grade)

Some completely blind children seem to be able to sense the color red. When one girl came to school in a red velvet dress, I automatically assumed she could too.

I called her to come close to the window. "Do you understand the color of this paper?" I asked, holding a red sheet in front of her eyes.

"No, I don't," she answered.

"What is the color of your dress?"

"Red."

"Hmm, you know its color. Do you like red?"

"What?"

"Isn't this paper the same color as your dress?"

"Huh?" She was still confused.

"How do you know the color of your dress?"

"My mother told me."

"I certainly beat around the bush with you, didn't I?"

I have seen some blind children really enjoy themselves waving red and gold sheets of paper in the sunlight very close to their eyes.

In addition, if one makes associations such as telling a blind child that white is as clean as snow and that black is the color used in funerals, he will think that white is a good color and black, a bad one.

A Car Driver (first grade)

Jiro, a congenitally blind first-grader, was a bright and cheerful boy. Even from a classroom on the third floor, he could tell when the milkman drove his car up to school.

Jiro and two weak-sighted children were discussing what they would do when they grow up.

"What are you going to be in the future?" one weak-sighted child asked the other.

"I want to be a bus driver."

"I want to be a car driver," Jiro asserted.

"But would it be safe for you to be one?" a friend asked him.

"I wouldn't ride in your car," another friend told him.

"Oh, what are you talking about! By the time I'm grown-up, I'll be really good," Jiro exclaimed.

"Well, if your eyes are open by then, you will."

"I wonder if they'll ever open," one weak-sighted child thought aloud.

"Of course they will open, they will open," Jiro stated quickly, trying to convince his friends.

Words I Cannot Forget (seventh grade)

"I'm so happy because you praised my artwork that I'd like to give you something," said a weak-sighted boy, handing me a clay candy bar. "I'm so pleased I won't be able to sleep tonight."

"If my eyes would open, only then would I be happy," interrupted a boy without eyes, a bitter tone to his voice.

I have never forgotten his words or the sudden change in atmosphere.

The Hand That Stuck to Me (second grade)

One girl came all the way from Kyushu and enrolled at our school. When she came for the first time, she was clinging tightly to her stepmother's hand. I understood that she had lost her sight because of a brain tumor, and that she had not very long to live.

I took her hand as she slowly climbed up the steps holding onto the handrail.

"*Sensei*, how come your hands are so rough?" she asked me.

I replied, "Because I work with clay all the time."

Even after we entered the classroom she didn't let go of my hand.

"*Sensei*, will you please still hold my hand tightly. Don't let go of me, please."

Even Though You Have Eyes (eighth grade)

When Goro began walking all the way to school with his cane, he looked much happier. Especially because he was born blind, this step must have made him more self-confident. Even so, he said he still got chills when very fine cars with quiet engines passed close by him.

"Oh, was I scared this morning! I have always been very sensitive to noises but that car — it was so quiet. I nearly got killed. Those big fine automobiles are our enemies. *Sensei*, be very, very careful. Even though you can see. If you were no longer here, then we'd really be in trouble."

The Scenery from Our Window (ninth grade)

Probably because of age, recently I began to notice I had trouble seeing at a distance. At noon recess, therefore, I look out at the distant trains and ships to strengthen my eyes.

One girl noticed me always standing by the window, and one

day she asked me what I was doing.

"I'm looking at trains and ships way out there," I explained to her.

"Oh, you're so lucky! I don't like your eyes at all."

"Oh, excuse me. I didn't mean to make you feel bad," I apologized.

The Eye Bank (fourth grade)

In recent years, eye contributions and banks as well as blood contributions and banks have become well known to the general public.

I told the children about this new system.

"Could I donate my eyes to the bank?" a blind boy asked.

"They'd say 'no thanks' to you. They only take good eyes," answered a boy who could see a little.

"I think I will give my eyes to someone when the time comes," I told them.

"*Sensei*, I suppose the person who receives your eyes will draw very good pictures."

"*Sensei*, when the time comes, I want your eyes first. All right? You promise me?"

"Then what would happen to *Sensei*?"

"He would no longer be living by that time," answered another girl.

Eye banks are places where the corneas of deceased donors are stored and given to those who will be able to see if they have cornea-transplant operations.

To See with My Soul (sixth grade)

Every blind child has suffered when playmates scorn them for being blind.

"*Sensei*, the kids in my neighborhood all call me 'blind,' " complained one boy.

"How do you answer them?" I asked.

"Well, why don't you just tell them there's nothing wrong with being blind," another blind boy answered for him.

"I always say, 'I didn't ask to be blind. If you want to say such cruel things, you should be blind yourself!' "

"Yes, but the kids in my neighborhood tell me they won't play with me unless I pay them," the first blind boy continued to complain.

"You shouldn't give up so easily. Tell them as I do that I see with my soul. How does that sound to you?"

"Perfect," replied a weak-sighted child, overhearing the conversation.

One's Life and One's Eyes (eighth grade)

I hear many sad stories about the suffering of families with children who have become blind. One mother said that she thought about committing suicide with her child after finding he was blind.* Another took her child on her back and went on a long pilgrimage of eighty-eight temples noted for healing on the island of Shikoku.

"Why I must be the one who is blind? My older brother has nothing wrong with *him*."

"Well, that's fate. I know it's hard but try to accept it and live with it," said a weak-sighted child rather sympathetically.

"My mother must have had a tough time with me when I was a baby. I heard she used to hide my face with her kimono so people wouldn't stare at me."

"When I was very little, the doctor told my parents that I wouldn't survive unless my eyes were taken out, because I had glioma of the retina, so, in a sense, I lost my eyes but in exchange for my life. So it's probably been relatively easy for me to accept my handicap. My mother still tells me sometimes that she feels sorry for what they had to do."

Changing Eyes (second grade)

A weak-sighted and a blind child were discussing their summer plans.

"I have to have another eye operation this summer. Nobody knows if my eyes will work better or not afterwards, but they say I've got to have it now. Operations are so painful, though, I just don't want to."

*Publisher's note: Strange as this may sound to the Western reader, this idea is not so uncommon in the Japanese way of thinking. It is seldom carried out, however.

"My mother told me that she would take me to the hospital after I finished fifth grade. Then she would have my bad eyes taken out and new ones put in."

This blind boy believes that his bad eyes may possibly be replaced with good eyes, not with glass eyes. His mother's suffering, hope, and love come through so clearly in his words.

Revenge for My Eyes! (fifth grade)

Some children forget to put eyes on their clay faces. Others don't want to.

Among the clay faces that do have eyes, some have eyeballs, some only hollows where eyes should be.

"I wonder if the clay figures we make need eyes?" Toyoji asked skeptically.

"Oh sure, they need them even if they are made by the blind," said his weak-sighted friend.

"All right, then. I'll give it a really good pair of deep-set eyes," Toyoji stated forcefully, jabbing two fingers into the face.

Happiness and Want (sixth grade)

Yuichi gets stronger every time someone scorns him for being blind. He is very competitive and even sheds tears if his artwork doesn't turn out as well as he thinks it should.

"If we all had the chance to have eye transplants, I don't think any of us would refuse them," a weak-sighted girl was telling a friend.

Yuichi said, "That's not so. Whatever you say, I say I don't want eyes. Once you get eyes, then you naturally want something else. Therefore, I'm content with what I have. I don't need anything. Don't confuse want with happiness!"

"You always rebel against everyone, don't you? You're probably in a bad mood because of the weather."

Drop Dead! (fifth grade)

When children start playing tag, it is a sign of approaching winter. To run at times like this, a weak-sighted child always takes the hand of a blind child, and they work together.

One such team of girls had just been tagged by "IT" because the blind girl was very slow and clumsy.

The weak-sighted girl was angry at her.

"You didn't run fast enough so they caught us. Shigechan, you should just drop dead!"

"Why should I? I like to live and I like to run, even though I can't do it as well as you can."

It Bugs Me (sixth grade)

Although many people have an image of the blind as always unhappy, most children at our school are very cheerful youngsters. Actually, instead of sympathy, these children need to be treated just as everyone else is. One student's comment clearly proves this.

"*Sensei*, since you can see, you may not understand this, but we don't really mind being blind. It just bugs me when people come up to me and say they feel sorry about my eyes."

Mother Would Never Die (third grade)

Parents of children at our school are always concerned about their sons' and daughters' futures. Naturally their children must rely on them far more than most people do.

"I hope my mother will live forty more years."

"I hope mine will live at least until I have my own children."

"My mom's gotta live three hundred more years."

"My mother said she would go after I die."

"Oh, Mommy will never die. She said she wouldn't be able to because she is so worried about me."

A Pencil Case with Flower Patterns (eighth grade)

Cornea transplants restore eyesight to ten per cent of the people who become blind. However, only a few students at schools such as ours are lucky enough to have such operations.

"How long, I wonder, do I have to stay blind? I became blind when I was seven years old, and I have lived with it since then. Why doesn't life work in such a way that someone would say, 'You've been such a good girl. You've never complained. So today

I will give you back your eyesight.' "

"I really wish I could see again. Then I could go buy a pencil case with flowers on it just like the one I used to have."

One boy quietly told himself, "I must put up with my blindness my whole life."

This dialogue took place among children who had lost their sight early in life.

Two Worlds (advanced class)

"In my head right here, I still have bullets from an antiaircraft gun." The forty-five-year-old blind man had them touch the battle scars on the back of his head.

The young audience was much impressed.

"Everybody here must think that blindness means that you only lose, that you gain nothing. Do you feel that way? Well, it's a big mistake to think so."

"You mean there's positive value to being blind?"

"Maybe I can offer you children a new point of view since I lost my sight in the middle of my life. In my case, I have lived in two worlds, the sighted as well as the sightless one. If you lose something as big as your eyes, then you're not so greedy about the rest of the world anymore. If you're not greedy, if you have very few desires, then don't you think that in the end you have become much richer? Since I've lost my eyesight, I have found I want very little. My wife guides me around hand in hand. I don't spend much money. I hear lots of music I never heard before and I don't have to witness horrible incidents. Thus, I have great peace of mind. Doesn't my life sound richer? This is what we call the blind man's heaven. Enough of my long lecture."

"Sir, you're a professional blind man, aren't you?"

Despair (eighth grade)

We received news from a doctor that Mitchan, who loves to paint, had a disease of the retina and that it was too late to save her gradually failing eyesight.

Five weak-sighted boys and girls and one blind boy were discussing her situation.

"I understand Mitchan will soon be blind. Poor Mitchan!"

"I wonder which is worse — losing your sight after you're born or being born blind."

"I wonder if it's possible to accept blindness if you have once been able to see."

"Yes, I wonder."

"If you are born blind, it wouldn't be so difficult, I suppose."

"Isn't it the desire to see that makes people suffer?"

"I wonder, if you are born blind, whether you have that desire."

The blind child could no longer keep quiet. "Oh, I want to see very much."

"Golly, if I became blind, I'd die in despair. Even geniuses like Beethoven thought of committing suicide when they became handicapped," commented one of the weak-sighted children.

"Then are you saying I'm stupid, because I don't think like Beethoven?" the blind boy concluded.

Deeper Through Our Touching (ninth grade)

One student lost his sight two years before. Talking with him one day, it struck me as perhaps important to find out how one feels in the critical period just before one becomes blind.

"Don't you think sighted people use their eyes very carelessly, because they know they can always look at things?"

"Yes, that's very true. In my case, I have only now. Since I think I can hear things only once, I'm all ears."

"Don't you think it easier to look at things with eyes?"

"Don't you think, *Sensei*, that we can perhaps look at things more deeply through touching?"

"Yes, you might be right."

"As my sight began to fail, I almost wished I would become blind overnight. At a time like that when you can see a little but you know you soon won't be able to see anything, you are so desperate that you can't settle down and focus on anything."

Marriage (adult)

One former student had come to visit me.

"*Sensei*, you remember Yochan? Well, she's marrying a man who can see. I don't think I would do that. *Sensei*, what do you think?"

"If you meet a fine person, I think you should get married. A real understanding of each other is more important than whether you or he can see. I know of only a few who have married sighted people, though."

"When even my own little brother sometimes gets frustrated with my slow pace, how can I expect anyone else to understand? Whatever people say, I think only the handicapped can really know how I feel."

"Yes, I agree with you."

"*Sensei*, would you seriously consider marriage with a blind person?"

"I might, but sympathy is not enough. One has to be attracted to another's personality as well. Do you know of anyone you like in that way?"

"I wonder if there's anyone who wants to marry me."

"Yes, I'm sure there is. Yochan is getting married. If you are receptive, there are many fine people in the world. You just can't sit around. You should be a little more outgoing and friendly. What's most important is to have confidence that you can handle a household."

"If I could only see just a little, my mother would feel so much better about my prospects of marriage."

"One thing you should keep in mind if you marry a blind person is whether or not his blindness is hereditary. You yourself, of course, don't have that worry."

"There's been talk of introducing me to some young men, but I worry. It seems lately a lot of men want a wife so they can be lazy. I don't like that."

"I wonder if there are really so many men who are that lazy."

"Even so, I'm still sort of scared of men who can see. Perhaps I'm over-sensitive right now since many of my friends are getting married."

"I think you'd be a fine wife since you are a loving person. Good luck to you."

"*Sensei*, why couldn't you have been born a little later?"

A Funny Question (second grade)

One cold afternoon I sat around the warm stove with some children and we talked about what they would be when they grow up.

"I want to be a pop singer. Then you'd be my fan, and come and listen to me."

"*Sensei*, when *you* grow up, what do you want to be?"

"Well, let's see . . . ."

Sensei Can See (third grade)

Because I sometimes take the children's hands to show them what I want to explain, sometimes they take my hand to show me their finished works.

"*Sensei*, it's well done, isn't it? Do you know what it is? This is the hand, this is the stomach . . ."

"Yes, you did a good job. I knew right away what it was even before you told me."

"Oh really? How?"

"I saw it, so I understood."

"Oh, that's right. *Sensei* can see."

If You Want Money (second grade)

Young children love to work in clay because they can make balls and sticks and call them whatever they want. They especially like candy, cookies, teacups, spoons, and flutes.

"Why can't I make something good in clay?" complained a weak-sighted boy.

"Because you're poor at it," said a blind girl abruptly.

"Someday I hope you all will make something more than just candies and fruit," I told the class.

"Oh, *Sensei*, I can make anything in clay. If you want money, I'll make you lots."

Heartless Adults

Our school gossip sessions are just like those of any other high school.

"I think there must be somebody you like. You've been acting kind of strange lately."

"What makes you say that?"

"I know, there is somebody, but you just won't tell me about him."

"You remember Akira really liked Takako. But since graduation you don't see them much together. These things don't seem to last very long, do they?"

"She was blind so, in the end, he left her. Men are so cruel, aren't they?"

"Well, women are cruel, too. My father's first wife deserted him, when he became blind. She said, 'I won't spend my time taking care of a blind man.' "

"Those love stories on TV aren't the real thing. Relationships like that only work when everything is going all right."

"I've the same sort of problem. My mother left my father, too, but I don't understand why. Could it have happened because I'm blind?"

"No, that isn't true. Your father must have been an irresponsible man."

The Soul (seventh grade)

One intelligent boy believes that a man's body and his soul are completely separate.

"*Sensei*, I think people live only when the soul likes them. If the soul decides it no longer likes a person, it says goodbye. Then, that is the end of that person. He dies. Everyone has to be loved by the soul."

The Words to Live By (ninth grade)

In schools for the blind throughout Japan, it seems, suicide is not uncommon.

"What is it that helps you live day by day?" I asked several of my blind students.

"When I think of my body as my own, I find it really hard to live. When I think of it as belonging to God, then it is easier."

"I don't think I should worry about my body. My heart is what I should be working on."

"It's useless to waste time thinking about your eyes. After all we still have hands, and ears. We just have to do our best with what we have."

"Recently I have begun to doubt whether I have the will to do anything in life. That's what's bothering me now."

"You suffer because you make comparisons. Just the way you are now is fine."

"I've never thought of doing a silly thing like committing suicide. They say when your eyes are closed, your heart will open. When it's really tough, talking it over with friends helps a great deal."

Voting in Braille (adults)

Tomorrow is Election Day. The blind adults here at the school go and vote in braille. After the election, when the votes are counted, teachers who can read braille are asked to interpret their ballots.

"I don't know whom I should vote for. Have you decided?"

"You remember Mr. Umio Yamano? I voted for him last time, since he had promised to work for the handicapped. But after the election he didn't do anything."

"If the Prime Minister or some great man's child had an eye problem, only then would they become interested."

Career Openings (seventh grade)

Only recently in our country have people become aware that the blind are seeking a wider range of jobs. Blind children dream of all sorts of job possibilities just as all children do.

"*Sensei*, why did you become a teacher?"

"Because I like children."

"When I grow up, I want to be a radio announcer."

"I want to be a stewardesss. They're great."

"Oh, I'm coming back here, to the school to teach."

"I wonder if even I could be a nurse."

"I think I'd like to be a mother."

"Yes, that's probably the very best."

"I don't want to grow up. I would hate that."

"How come?"

"I must take over my father's business."

"Then you mean you'd be a masseur?"

"Guess what I'd be if I could see?"

"Oh, in your case, do you really think it matters?"

Spring Window (sixth grade)

Sitting by the window looking out at the harbor on a fine spring day, I heard this conversation between a weak-sighted boy and a completely blind boy.

"Do you remember when your eyes began to fail?"

"Well, I wasn't born with eyes."

"Oh, really?"

"When my mother was carrying me, she didn't have enough to eat because it was wartime."

"Then we are both victims of the war."

"It wasn't my mother's fault. She did her best to make a healthy boy but the war. . . ."

Right after World War II, a number of people in their sixties enrolled in our school. One old man confessed that "all of us here thought at least once about committing suicide when we found out we were blind." What kept them going was the understanding and support of their loved ones, just like the devoted mother of the child without eyes.

This is All Right (fourth grade)

A cute little girl brought me a childlike human figure with a small flat face and no facial features.

"*Sensei*, is this all right? This is an angry child."

"Huh, it's well done but where are the eyes?"

"It doesn't matter whether she has them, she's all right as she is." She forcefully pushed away my hand.

For a long time after this, she would never put eyes in the faces of her figures nor would she tell why. I found out from her grandmother that she had had an unsuccessful eye operation.

A Treasure Box (eighth grade)

When the eight-graders do woodwork, they like to make special treasure boxes for keeping their own secret things.

"Mutsumi, what are you going to make?" a weak-sighted boy asked a blind boy.

"I want to make a treasure box. It's for love letters and things like that, you know."

"What are you saying? Since you can't see, how can you make a box?"

"I knew you'd say that. That shows the limits of sighted people."

As a rule, contrary to what might be expected, blind children do better in woodwork than weak-sighted children who tend to rely only on their sight, however little it may be. Blind children carefully listen for the ring of a nail as they strike it into the wood, and by the vibrations and sounds, they know whether it's gone in straight or not.

The Day of an Eye Operation (sixth grade)

There are very few whose eye operations are successful among the children who have enrolled in schools like ours. Occasionally, however, there is a story with a happy outcome, but the other students don't really know how to accept it.

"Right now Tokiko is probably having her cataract operation. I wonder how it'll turn out."

"I heard she has a really good chance of seeing again."

"I'm so envious. Why won't I be able to see someday too? I've had many operations, but I still can't see. It just isn't fair."

"I want an operation, too," sighed the only completely blind boy in the group.

"I wonder if you ever would be able to see?"

"No, and I know that."

Sightseeing in Kobe (fifth grade)

Just in the few years since they built a subway in Kobe, the city has rapidly changed in appearance.

"There's a subway stop in my neighborhood now. They say the trams are disappearing. What am I going to do? I feel as if my house got up one morning and walked to a new neighborhood. Unless I keep track of all the changes going on around here, I won't know where any place is," a weak-sighted girl complained to some blind friends.

"Then, when I can see someday, I want you to take me around and show me everywhere in Kobe."

"Oh, I don't want eyes that can just see Kobe. I want eyes that can see all the way to America."

I Want a Picture Book that My Hands Can See (fifth grade)

We received a donation of old picture books for the weak-sighted. I felt sorry for the blind child who was trying to get the attention of her weak-sighted friend engrossed in one of them.

"What are you doing? Aren't you going to play with me? Well, at least talk to me."

Not lifting her head, the friend murmured, "I'm looking at a picture book."

"Is it so interesting that you can't even answer me? Show it to me, too."

"Oh, you haven't seen them yet? Take a look."

"Hmm, so this is the picture book. My neighbor Mitchan takes these things to kindergarten sometimes. I wonder what she does with them. I want a picture book that my hands can see."

These words inspired me to develop a new kind of picture books for blind children. They are fairy tales written in braille and illustrated with pictures that have special raised surfaces.

To design these pictures, I relied heavily on blind children's paintings I have collected over the years. Naturally these pictures are quite different from those in ordinary picture books. Wherever possible, I have tried to use scraps of materials that resemble or are part of the real objects themselves, for example, a feather to show an ostrich, a piece of satin cloth to show a princess's gown.

Big Hands (fourth grade)

Akio had already finished a really fine piece of work, and had gone to the washroom to clean up.

"Akio went to wash his hands such a long time ago and he's still not back yet. What's he doing in there?"

"Isn't he just washing his hands really well?"

"He must have enormous hands."

Many people think that all blind people are gloomy in outlook, but it isn't so.

Infinite Light (sixth grade)

Why are some children blind? That is a question only God can answer. All I know is how little I am able to do for them as a teacher.

"*Sensei*, because you've done good things, I know you'll go to heaven," said a girl who had lost her sight in the middle of her childhood.

"No, you're the one that will go to heaven. I know God already wants you there."

"When we both get to heaven, then I'll be able to see you with my eyes."

"Yes, yes, I'm sure that will happen."

Praying
by Yoko Masaoka (first-grade girl)

The big eye-hollows are empty, and the hands are pressed in prayer, but they are folded without power.

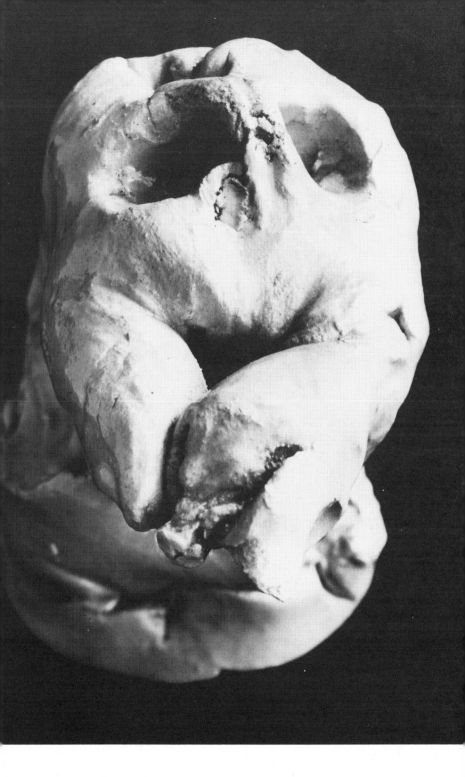

About the Author

Shiro Fukurai was born in Kobe in 1920. In 1933, he graduated from Hyogo Prefecture Engineering School in Mechanics. He started to work as a designer but soon left due to illness. After his recovery, he became a substitute teacher at a primary school. He was drafted into the army in 1942 and served in China. In the chaos following World War II, he did a variety of jobs, teaching, earning an acupuncture license, and working as a designer on a newspaper. In 1950, he became a teacher for the blind as recounted in this book.

Among his achievements as an art instructor for the blind and weak-sighted are:

"The Exhibition of Lightless Sculptors" held in major Japanese cities (1957).

The film "The Children of the Dark" received a Minister of Education Prize in the Japan Educational Films Festival (1959).

A Yomiuri-TV documentary film, "What Is It Like to See?" received a special prize in the annual TV Drama Festival (1961).

The Art Exhibit "What Is It Like to See?" held in major Japanese cities (1962).

The booklet of brush drawings, "Standing on Our Own Feet, " sent to institutes for the handicapped in over seventy countries (1965).

A new kind of picture books designed especially for the blind introduced on NHK-TV (1966).

Hoping to contribute his share to international understanding, Mr. Fukurai has sent his students' works to many parts of the world.

He hopes to introduce his students' works in exhibitions abroad, once he has collected enough money to finance this project.

Mr. Fukurai's current projects at his school include teaching the weak-sighted how to do wood-block prints. He is most concerned about the futures of his students and envisions ways of making their lives easier, such as setting up a blind and retarded children's institute and a nationwide system of young adult centers for the blind.